Listening to Our Bodies

Listening to Our Bodies

The Rebirth of Feminine Wisdom

Stephanie Demetrakopoulos

Beacon Press   Boston

Grateful acknowledgment is made for permission to reprint from the following: "Monster" from *Monster* by Robin Morgan, copyright © 1972, by permission of Random House, Inc. *The Stone Angel* by Margaret Laurence, copyright © 1964, by permission of Alfred A. Knopf, Inc. *Song of Solomon* by Toni Morrison, copyright © 1977, by permission of Alfred A. Knopf, Inc. "Morning Song" and "Words" from *The Collected Poems: Sylvia Plath*, edited by Ted Hughes, copyright © 1961 by Ted Hughes, by permission of Harper & Row, Publishers, Inc. and Olwyn Hughes. *My Mother's House; and Sido* by Colette, copyright © 1953, by permission of Farrar, Straus & Giroux, Inc. "Tampons" from *For Earthly Survival* by Ellen Bass, copyright © 1980 by Moving Parts Press, by permission of Ellen Bass. *The Evening Star* by Colette, copyright © 1973, by permission of Peter Owen Ltd.: Publishers and copyright © 1974 by Colette, used by courtesy of the Bobbs-Merrill Publishing Co., Inc. "The Consecrating Mother" from *45 Mercy Street* by Anne Sexton, copyright © 1976, by permission of Houghton Mifflin Company. "Seventh Psalm," "Ninth Psalm" and "The Fury of Guitars and Sopranos" from *The Death Notebooks* by Anne Sexton, copyright © 1974, by permission of Houghton Mifflin Company. Early versions of chapter 3, "The Nursing Mother and Feminine Metaphysics," and chapter 4, "The Older Woman as Matriarch," will appear in *Soundings* and as "Life Stage Theory, Gerontological Research, and the Mythology of the Older Woman: Independence, Autonomy, and Strength" in *Anima*, vol. 8, no. 2, Spring 1982.

Beacon Press books are published under the auspices of the Unitarian Universalist Association of Congregations in North America, 25 Beacon Street, Boston, Massachusetts 02116
Published simultaneously in Canada by
Fitzhenry & Whiteside Limited, Toronto

Printed in the United States of America

(hardcover) 9 8 7 6 5 4 3 2 1
(paperback) 9 8 7 6 5 4 3 2 1

Library of Congress Cataloging in Publication Data

Demetrakopoulos, Stephanie, 1937–
   Listening to our bodies.

   Bibliography: p.
   Includes index.
   1. Women — Psychology. 2. Life cycle, Human.
3. Women — Physiology. I. Title.
HQ1206.D363 1982   305.4   81-70489
ISBN 0-8070-6704-0   AACR2
ISBN 0-8070-6705-9   (pbk.)

6-4-85

To my husband, Yorgo, whose devotion and commitment to me as a friend, a husband, and a fellow intellectual in the midst of often difficult family situations provide my ground of being. More than anyone else in my life he has had to put up with the moodiness, the fatigue, and the night terrors that came with my writing this book.

To my mother, Alice Richardson, from whom I learned a passion for justice, the virtues of endurance and on-goingness, and a love of learning.

To my father, Charles Richardson, who, in spite of a fragmented, difficult background of his own, has provided continuity and security for his family.

To my children Luan, Natasha, and Yorgo, who immeasurably enrich and deepen my life, try my soul, and help me grow, usually by turning out to be more than I expected.

To my stepchildren, Harvey, Anna, Thea, and Dimitri, from and for whom I have learned hard and valuable lessons about loving.

To my mothers-in-law, Florence Treece and Dorothy Fisher, and my mother's lifelong friends Kay Clark, Mary Jo Dodge, Louise Thomas and Margo Linden. These women embody (with my own mother) inspirational images of strong and unique older women that have been and will be a lifelong study for me.

To my grandmother Elsie Hays, long dead, but whose gnarly — even ornery — eccentricity is remembered and influential still in all her descendants.

To my loving friend, Cary Woods, who will also always be missed.

Acknowledgments

I hereby acknowledge the Western Michigan University Faculty Award which allowed me time for working on this manuscript; the Research Services Department of Western Michigan also volunteered typing services when the English Department secretaries were over-burdened. I am indebted mostly, however, to the typing skills and patience of Linda Fortino, Diane Allen, Janet Dines, and Charlotte True.

I am thankful to Robert Sardello who first urged me to put this material into book form after reading the first chapters as separate essays. Other friends who read and commented helpfully on early drafts of chapters are Caren Dybek, Diane Seuss, Shirley Scott, and Jaimy Gordon. Edward Griffin critiqued several of my essays over the years; besides his slaying the dragon so I could finish my doctorate, he inculcated whatever writing skills I have achieved. My editor Joanne Wyckoff has re-shaped the entire manuscript several times in order to give the book form and integrity; she has moreover remained encouraging and cheerful in the face of even the most chaotic revisionings. The second editor for Beacon Press, Liz Duvall, pared, sharpened, and focused many sections with great rigor.

Without the excellent childcare which gave me the precious time blocks to write, there is, of course, no way I could have written this book. I can never thank these women enough for the warm, nurturing care they have given my children: Dorothy Bainbridge, Jenny Dewolf, Jean Bishop, the staff at the Canterbury Day Care Center, especially Sally Householder.

Certain chapters owe much to discussions and the influence of certain friends and colleagues. JoAnn Moody first started me thinking about the image of women in literature, especially the older woman; Marilyn Bell's class on the older woman further influenced my researching both that topic and women's attitudes toward death. John Murphy helped me years ago to see how differently black women often live out feminine archetypes; the chapter on Toni Morrison owes much to discussions with him. Many other friends have been essential to helping me see more deeply into women's problems and life patterns; among them are Joan Khaled, John Orr, Elaine Jayne, Michael Richardson, Donna Carol, Katy Cooney, Amy Demetrakopoulos, Vi Murphy, Barb Hoekzema, Toni and Frank Gross, Susan Hannah, Carol Larson, Jill Cohn, Sally Putney, Clare Goldfarb, Karla Holloway, Rita Verbrugge, Donna Eisenberg, Marilyn Miller, Theone Hughes, Carol Norman, Helene Kountanis, Tom Bailey, Bob Hinkel, Judy Gay, Maria Corakis, Kathy Drzick, and Marjorie Palmer-Burns. The sections on women's spirituality were greatly influenced by my friend and in-the-flesh spirit guide Ann Hardin Strauss.

Certain students who are dear to me and whose ideas were also seminal forces in my thought must also be named; among them are Janet Harsch, Linda Valdez, Genna Southworth. And finally I want to thank the women (Polly, Brenda, Sarah, Karen) at the Yarn Merchant for therapy they have unwittingly provided.

Preface

Women's philosophy and theology are just beginning to emerge publically. The recent polls that show how much more women reject warmongering leaders than do men are an expression of women's philosophy as well as a political statement. Part of the women's movement has been a strong defense of persons politically disenfranchised, unable to speak for themselves—children, displaced housewives, women on welfare. The women's movement has embraced Third World women, lesbian women; part of the movement's ongoing moral struggle has been its care to include all persons. This is the way women's philosophy has generally manifested itself—in behavior; this behavior in the past has been basic to the private sector of life, the home. Men have made it the fulcrum of their homecoming, their haven. Now as women begin to have a public voice and to influence the world outside the home, as they begin to work within and help expand the structures of patriarchal institutions, they need as never before verbal accounts of their philosophy. This book attempts to show how matriarchal wisdom differs from patriarchal and how much the world needs matriarchal wisdom. After reading this book women should realize anew how crucial their presence is in the world outside their homes, though their presence in the home and family can never be truly estimated or appreciated.

A term I use frequently throughout this book is the verb "to sacralize," which some readers, conservative about language, may object to as a neologism. I could use "to make sacred" instead, but I simply need the verb without the noun because I think the verbal expression of women's spirituality is in a state of process, of beginnings, at this time. To fully understand the subtitle of this book, "The Rebirth of Feminine Wisdom," remember that renaissance means rebirth. But as in the first great Renaissance, this renaissance gives new form and dynamism to that which is born again. While I look at ancient goddesses lost to modern women's consciousness, such as Demeter or Artemis, to deepen into the past and significance of women, I see that modern women are re-enacting these archetypes with greater complexity. Modern women are also bringing a new consciousness to the wisdom of these archetypes and perhaps even creating and living out new archetypes.

The word "bodies" in the title must also be read broadly. Modern women must be careful not to become lost from their own best feminine wisdom—the wisdom of the body—especially those women who work in fields dominated by men. This book also develops women's relationships to "bodies" of thought that originate from a woman's experiences of her own body and that derive from woman's connection to the collective body of the matriarchy. A third female body important to this book is the Earth Herself, whose presence to women as a deity is best developed by Susan Griffin in *Woman and Nature*. As developed in Chapter I, lesbian communities especially revere and live close to this Mother Body.

The methodology of this book reflects my life and my studies, often delved into to understand my life better. Due to multiple marriages and many children and stepchildren, I have been all my life steeped in different family situations and questioned the meaning of family for myself and other women. I have also been steeped in literature, art, psychology, philosophy and theology and I bring these disparate disciplines to bear throughout this book.

Literature and art have always been central to my life because I think ultimate meaning resides in image not concept, though I would not have written this book if the struggle to verbalize the image were not also in my opinion central to the quest for truth. One of the reasons that I chose to devote my doctoral studies to Renaissance literature and art was my sense of that period as reflecting a joy in fecundity and plenitude, a merging of spirituality and sexuality, and a sense of the complexity of nature/nurture—all crucial forces in my life as a woman. After graduate school I studied different perspectives of depth psychology, Freudian and Jungian, especially the latter which affords a metaphysics of depth imagery. I spent a number of years studying images of the feminine as generated by women authors and artists and as illuminated by depth psychology. I use literature as vehicle, as quasi-case study, for the theories developed in this book. I also spent about two years studying gerontology to better understand the last stages of women's lives. Readings in philosophy and theology have helped me develop and broaden my theories on the feminine.

This book, then, is interdisciplinary. I hope the richness I've tried to bring to it can give women insight into what it means to exist within the body of woman.

Contents

I
THE PHYSICAL BODY

This first section considers how a woman's sojourn incarnated in a female body affects her. Chapter I analyzes how women's early adult life stages influence their maturation into adults. The next two chapters consider the wisdom and soul growth possible from two specifically female body functions — birth and breast-feeding. Chapter IV focuses on the experience of old age as a woman consolidates these earlier experiences into matriarchal wisdom. Since death is the crux, the enigma, that most puzzles mortals in discovering their place in the universe and in finding meaning in their lives, I end this section with Chapter V, women's attitudes toward death, the final feminine transformation. In this section I show how women move through nature, through their bodies, to a spirituality that is far less dualistic than men's traditionally has been.

1. Becoming an Adult

For a number of reasons I think that women are more moral than men. They commit far fewer crimes than men, and the crimes they do commit are usually not violent. Without benefit of theory, theology, or expostulation that describes their lives, women have almost always behaved morally and responsibly to those who depend on them. The major evidence for this assertion is simply the survival of the species. Males may monopolize the technology of medicine, but women still do the nursing. Women have always cared for the young, the old, and the sick. Without receiving any kind of fame or credit for it (after all, it's "natural," so why praise "innate" behaviors that merely take all a person's strength and time), they have mothered the young, and other dependents, often under literally killing circumstances. And then women are made to feel they are lesser creatures for never articulating (that is, posturing, pontificating) about the philosophy they have lived out.

The basic reason that women live more morally and less violently, aggressively, and theoretically than men is their unique ego development. To consider ego development, we must consider life-stage theories, all of which take men as their norm. I do not intend to offer a formula or set theory of women's life stages, partly because I am not sure that is possible or even desirable. I will consider certain crucial ways in which women's psychology and development differ from life-stage theory that centers on male norms. I also want to suggest the complexity of forces in women's lives and the way that these often shape women's development differently from men's. While I give some attention to earlier life stages of women in this book, I am most interested in adult life stages, so I emphasize post-adolescence in this chapter.

Usually considered the first modern and foremost life-style theorist, Erik Erikson offers a good primary ground for my dissent. Erikson formulates eight stages of psychosocial development:

1. Trust versus mistrust. The infant learns enough trust in its caretakers to sustain its faith in the universe it has recently entered.
2. Autonomy versus shame, guilt. The toddler develops a sense of separateness and self-will.
3. Initiative versus guilt. The preschooler learns more autonomy and faith in self.
4. Industry versus inferiority. The school-aged child gradually learns a sense of competence and hence self-esteem.
5. Identity versus identity confusion. The adolescent develops a sense of self in society that will carry him throughout all adult responsibilities and commitments. The birth of the ego occurs here for Erikson.
6. Intimacy versus isolation. The person rediscovers the importance of relationship versus the career for which the previous stages have prepared him.
7. Generativity versus stagnation. The fully developed person (able to be intimate as well as to achieve) produces his greatest contributions to society.
8. Integrity versus despair. The old person continues his ideological commitment to the world and stoically fends off despair in the face of death.[1]

The reader will notice that I use masculine pronouns from stage five on because Erikson is in reality talking about men's development specifically and conclusively from that stage on.

The ego not only emerges within a different chronology for women, but the relationship between the ego and the self is probably different throughout women's life stages. Various depth psychologists (archetypalists, Freudians, Jungians) distinguish between the ego and the self in a way that is helpful here. Think of the ego as the tip of an iceberg that surfaces out of the oceanic unconscious; this consciousness, the separate and autonomous ego, recedes and resurges in and out of sleep, where it is nourished and buffeted by the forces of the unconscious. The self is all the forces of the personality, those that lie dormant in the unconscious and manifest in later stages of life, the sum total of the contents and mysteries of the unconscious (collective and personal) as well as ego consciousness. For Erikson, this ego emerges with clear boundaries and oppositions against both the unconscious and other persons during adolescence. I do not think that women's egos ever become as severely cut off as young males' from the forces of the self or other people. As I shall prove, the very quality of the emerging and perhaps more dynamic feminine ego is different. The tendrils or, more negatively, tentacles of telepathic and other unconscious connections are not as harshly repressed in feminine ego development.

Erikson tends to see the first five life stages as gradual separation from the family and movement into the community; after establishing a career, a person moves on to the sixth life stage, which involves a search for intimacy. Erikson claims to be speaking about both sexes, but his prose constantly betrays that the pronoun *he* really does mean a male. Erikson consistently sees quite deeply into men's problems during mid-life, ages thirty-five to forty-five. It is important to remember that his theory of life stages rests on Freud's theory of the Oedipus complex, as do most other life-stage theories—so much so that it seems that Freud did, rather unerringly, define a central source of male anxiety, perhaps more an anxiety of adult males than of the young child. This seems apparent in certain research on men's projection of Oedipal patterns onto their sons, although clinical studies of little boys do not find these patterns. [2] As children, boys do not seem to hate their fathers, wish to usurp the mother's sexual love, or to topple the authority of the father. But as grown sons, adult males seem angry toward their fathers. Interestingly, Freud came to theorize about the Oedipus complex through his own anger, as a grown man, at his father. I wonder if there is not often, though repressed, an anger toward fathers in many grown sons because of the relative absence of those fathers in their childhood, which means the sons flounder toward gender consciousness with no loving, nurturing male models or support. They then become angry in turn with their own sons for usurping the only source of love they have been able to count on, the wife as surrogate mother. Daughters, of course, can become surrogate mothers to their fathers, so they are less threatening. Thus, anger at often unreasonable standards of achievement for men and a concomitant lack of fatherly love or attention in men's lives may underlie Erikson's theory of life stages.

Because cultures generally force a boy to relinquish his mother earlier plus more sharply and irrevocably than a girl must, many adult men grow up feeling overwhelmingly lonely and bereft (especially if their fathers were not very nurturing, which unfortunately is more typical than not.) I have written elsewhere of the fate of sons in a household where the mother identifies almost exclusively with her daughters and the father is absent, either physically or emotionally. Studies of rapists reveal that they grew up feeling on the periphery of their families and behaved as loners throughout their school years. Their anger toward women seems to come from a sense of separation. There is a great clientele for sadomasochistic activities among politically powerful and affluent men, which may reflect their need for pain in order to be sure that they and the Other (feminine values? women?) really exist.

As Erikson notes, men can become lost in the role structures of whatever institutions they choose to spend their lives in; too soon they cannot touch ground:

> If the times favor an impersonal kind of interpersonal pattern, a man can go far, very far, in life and yet harbor a severe character problem doubly painful because he will never feel really himself, although everyone says he is "somebody."[3]

Such men must feel like the subjects of experiments in which people are placed in deprivation tanks where their senses are all cut off. They cannot reach through their role to another person, and so they are fixated in an emotionally killing separation. Of course, they yearn back toward their mothers and, forgivably, want to kill the fathers who invented the terrible system in which they are lost and from which they cannot easily escape.

Social scientists have not even begun to fathom the amount of alienation, pain, and grief men suffer in the life stages that our culture finds "normal." Probably the researchers themselves, almost all male until recent years, are as out of touch with their wounds as their subjects are. But consider the symptoms of masculine pathology, the terrible acting out in rape, war, murder, and mutilation of excruciating internal imagery. Phyllis Chesler in her book *About Men* has gathered together some terrifying newspaper accounts of these male-generated atrocities.

Much of the woundedness in men is due to emotionally killing forms of enculturation visited upon little boys. Consider the severe beatings and physical abuse they often receive, the insistence (in public schools, for example)[4] that they behave as quietly, sedately, and with as much concentration as girls (who seem to mature earlier in all cultures), and the pressure that they conform to a brutalizing soldier or macho male role model, reinforcing male aggression. There may also be innate forces in the male psyche that make the pattern of lonely separateness a natural one for many men. Certainly their greater aggression may impel them into competitive, isolating modes of life. But even if some of these forces are innate, our culture has not even begun to find ways to soften them, to help little boys become conscious of these forces so that they may control and thus reap positive fruits from their masculinity.

The great urgency connected with masculine lack of self-knowledge, of course, is that it seems to be threatening the very existence of life on this planet. The education of young males needs the closest scrutiny. In Michigan, a recent study shows that the bulk of physical punishment inflicted by teachers is directed toward black male students. Why is it that over 90 percent of the children who are diagnosed as hyperactive are male? Do competitive sports provide an outlet for male aggression, or do they encourage it? Should males be given more time to play during school hours or have more rigorous physical workout periods during the school day? Perhaps more male than female children need intense moral education, for where there is more physical strength and aggression, there is surely a stronger need for restraint. More awareness of moral goals, of protective gentleness as an end in itself, should perhaps be deliberately inculcated in boys. While this book is concerned with the redemption, celebration, and further naming of the feminine, men may finally be in direr straits than women. Since their development is considered the norm, far less questioning and change in the treatment of young boys goes on than with young girls. This may be the greatest blind spot in our time, what Suzanne Langer calls the unquestioned yet false premise from which all other philosophical questions are asked.[5] Sharper definitions of what women are and are not may help in this great need to redefine, to really see, the masculine.

Perhaps Erik Erikson's life stages will be found to pertain to the women who never marry or never have children and instead pursue careers as singlemindedly as most men do. But even here, complexities arise. Among lesbians, for example, the second and third stages Erikson names—autonomy vs. shame, and doubt/initiative vs. guilt—are especially difficult because of the public stigma that their sexual choice carries. They certainly face stage five, identity vs. identity confusion, with less certain role models and with greater pressures and more difficulty than the average male heterosexual upon whom Erikson based his study. On the other hand, older lesbians probably have greater ease in passing through stage six, which Erikson marks as the later life-stage crisis of undeveloped eros or personal intimacy. Lesbian women who have married men and had children or who have undergone artificial insemination probably experience many of the same life stages as their heterosexual counterparts. The impact of children on a woman's life is deeper and more irrevocable than the impact of whatever life partner she may choose, although in the years when the children finally leave home, this may change.

Celeste, in Rita Mae Brown's novel *Six of One*, suggests an interesting life pattern for an upper-class lesbian woman. She conceives a grand passion during her college years for a woman whose artistic drive and social-climbing ambitions turn out to be antithetical to the life Celeste chooses to return to—a domestic but involved life in her small community, Runnymede. Celeste develops and sustains for her whole life a monogamous relationship with a second lover, Ramelle. Yet at a point in mid-life when she plunges into a metaphysical despair, Celeste goes to the home of her illiterate older maid, a mother and wise woman who takes Celeste into her bed and embraces the fear out of her being. The women do not relate erotically, yet the imagery of these nude female bodies entwined alone in the night, one the mother, the other the lost and pained daughter, has a merging, consoling quality. Feminine resources of love may be more available to the lesbian than to the straight woman as she moves through different life stages.

A more negative treatment of the monogamous life-style of many lesbians is found in Djuna Barnes's *Nightwood*. Nora, a rather dried-out intellectual, follows Robin, who represents Nora's connection to her unconscious, to mystery, to the animal within. A strange, primordial Neanderthal of a woman, Robin forever flees Nora, who stands as a higher form of individuation which she cannot and does not wish to achieve. Barnes's view of life is so dark that one scarcely thinks it exists. Far more typical is the love that continues to exist between lesbian women after an erotic relationship ends.

This passionate understanding is powerfully portrayed in Adrienne Rich's book of poems *The Dream of a Common Language*. Rich's book also portrays two aspects of feminine culture that lesbian women seem to be more acutely conscious of than many heterosexual women are. The first is an awareness of our foremothers and their lost culture; the second, an attachment to the earth as a goddess-form and an image of the bedrock that woman is to the species—walked on, unappreciated, freely exploited, but also strong and enduring. The Earth Mother as a spiritual resource is central to many lesbian women's metaphysics. They celebrate Christmas as a winter-solstice festival based on the promise of spring rather than as a centerpiece of a male-directed religion. I have on my desk a Christmas card from a lesbian couple. On its front is a woman with a heart-shaped womb out of which emerges a Christlike figure framed by a white tree and black tree which echo yin and yang (feminine and masculine) polarities; the inscription on the card reads, "May the rebirth of the Light bring you all good things." Many lesbian women follow a diet that hearkens back to more matriarchal times when the fruits of the earth itself, the women's gathering—rather than the prey of the men's hunting—was the chief supply of food.[6] Some lesbians celebrate the solstices with ritual ceremonies in their homes—a practice that surely sharpens their awareness of the seasons and the cyclical passage of time. There is strong evidence that lesbian culture has developed patterns that could possibly benefit us all, but no one has yet studied their life stages in depth.

Even straight women's sexuality is often not as thoroughgoing as men's. Both Anaïs Nin and Colette, whom I discuss later, had lesbian relationships that, though short-lived, seemed essential to their development. There may be complexities and depths in women's sexual patterns that have yet to be explored.

BIRTH OF THE FEMININE EGO

Mythic patternings and stories of childhood scarcely exist for women. Stories about the childhoods of the Greek gods abound, but little is available about the childhoods of such goddesses as Aphrodite, Demeter, Artemis, and Hestia. We must look mainly to modern fiction and nonfiction of women to find out how little girls individuate, experience adolescence, and become women.

If the boy is father to the man, as Wordsworth said, is the girl mother to the woman? How should we become adults? Kill a bear, join a law firm, prove ourselves in single combat? The best recent book that attempts to find underlying patterns that lead to womanhood is *The Reproduction of Mothering: Psychoanalysis and the Sociology of Gender* by Nancy Chodorow. She describes how little girls' lives predispose them toward their unique gender patterns. She speaks of this as a pattern that reproduces mothers. Chodorow shows how the "more permeable ego membrane" of the feminine psyche is subtly inculcated through a longer and closer attachment to the mother than boys experience. Thus, the propensity for love and deep attachment to another, plus a tendency to overidentify with the love object, to be unable to discern clearly where the other person leaves off and she begins, predestine a woman to what I call "grand passion" as the salient force of her first stage of adulthood (analogous to Erikson's stage five). I think this central impetus for love, eros, and relatedness is innate in women; Chodorow seems to think it is all enculturated. Whether it is enculturated or not is beside the point. It simply is.

The facelessness of a woman's first love is mythically presented in the lovely and intricate tale of Cupid and Psyche, in which Psyche marries Cupid, meets and makes love with him only in the dark, and enjoys him as a faceless lover for a long time.[7] Then her curiosity makes her light a torch to see him. Neither she nor he can bear the fall from love that his becoming an individual entails; he flees, and she must develop special strengths through a series of tasks in order to get him back. This tale nicely describes the facelessness of a woman's first gender consciousness and how her worth seems to ride on her conformity with his anima needs—her lover's expectations that she will be his ideal image of woman.[8]

Since falling in love is largely a transpersonal involvement of unconscious forces and since women intuit their mates' projections more accurately and often desire more deeply to conform with them, this experience, though euphoric, is often extremely painful for the woman, from her attempt to fit herself to the man's projections to the gradual withdrawing of projections by each person if the relationship is to grow and continue. Because the first great love contains the full force of the animus archetype, of the women's image and need for the inner and outer masculine, her emotions are so hazy, abstract, nonverbal, nebulous, and surging from such depths that her pain and grief (as the relationship begins to "fall" and change or even end) is free-floating and cannot be easily contained and controlled. Some women become awash in it and feel they will die of it.

There are many renditions of the first "grand passion" and they need not be only heterosexual, even for the heterosexual. In her first diary, Anaïs Nin recounts falling in love with June Miller, whom Henry Miller described to her as his muse. Building June up as the ideal woman, Nin fell in love with her before they had even met — she fell in love with the anima of the most creative and encouraging male artist she knew. Colette probably fell in love with her first husband, Willy, as a representation of her writer self, as did Sylvia Plath with Ted Hughes. Unknown parts of the self may get entangled in love relationships when the woman is young and has yet to realize her talents or career.

Women who marry young very often enter marriage with a desire for a purity of self to be found in and through their husbands. Women ponder and meditate over love and marriage far more than men do. (Erikson remarks that only men who are specially gifted or weak — his words — specialize in that "inwardness and sensitive indwelling [the German *Innigkeit*] usually ascribed to women."[9]) The woman's total attachment to her husband and new marriage, so often quickly followed by a child, distinguishes feminine ego development from its masculine counterpart. Usually, then, a woman's young-adult years are steeped and grounded in relatedness and the contingencies of others. Yet her romantic idealism often engenders a sense of personal failure and humiliation. As Judith Bardwick, a writer on the psychology of women, points out, it is far easier to measure success in the career world than in the friction and ambivalence of family relationships. Certainly husbands, after women forego the impossibly ideal projections they usually conceive initially, turn out to be fallible, vulnerable persons, as human as any of us. Many young women entering into marriage state proudly that their home, marriage, children, husband, will never be as flawed as their mothers'. Yet all marital relationships go through the fall over and over; and all children, being individual humans, are not what we expect or shape them to be. A woman thus faces an arduous process of painful readjustment and plain hard work in her everyday domestic and personal life. This makes it difficult for her in later years to imagine or live life as if it were lightly achieved or to be looked at from only one's own perspective. She must adjust or realign her ideals downward to the reality of what actual relationships bring.

Thus, women have greater expectations for marriage than do men who, besides possessing less permeable ego membranes, and being less emotionally vulnerable, spread their expectations into realms other than family life. This is one reason that young women should have at least a part-time job, no matter how many small children they have. Trips into the outside world and interaction with other adults keep the domestic life in perspective and help to alleviate and dilute the inevitable difficulties and disappointments. Even if women work full-time, they are almost always much more involved with the emotional development of their preschool children than their husbands are. This seems to be changing, but I doubt that many men will ever be as patient and long-suffering with small children as most women are. I agree with Dorothy Dinnerstein that the presence of men in the nursery is a revolution to be desired, but I think most men simply have less tolerance for the ambiguity and nonrational elements of young children.[10] Women too have to learn patience, but they generally have more innate endurance for the kinds of stress infants and toddlers create.

Thus women who marry and/or have children at a young age undergo an extended self-abnegation and service to total dependents. This is a slow and exceedingly drawn-out death of whatever narcissistic egoism they have achieved in adolescence (early in Erikson's fifth stage, when identity and ego coalesce for men). The first marriage (sometimes the only one) to the aggressive, demanding, and generally less considerate young husband, the first child with its total claim on the daily life and even the sleep of its mother — these are initiation rites that most women have undergone (especially in the past). By the time these women reach their mid-thirties, whatever ego they have left is solid, self-assured, and buffeted smooth. This gradual process by which a woman's self is born is quite different from what shapes the young, fifth-stage male's flying, unattached ego, who takes for granted his place as the breadwinner, the career-maker, because the wife will carry most of the weight of making the relationship and marriage work. Her ego must grow; she must develop confidence to become a full human being. His ego must diminish and make room for others. It is interesting in this regard to note the statistics that indicate how many more women than men are willing to enter marriage counseling, and how many more women end up initiating divorce. Both examples suggest that women carry the responsibility for the quality of the marriage.

The self-sacrifice that women so often seem to experience in the earlier years is most colorfully and vividly seen in Colette's first marriage, as described in her *My Apprenticeships*. Many of her biographers exclaim wonderingly over why she spent all those years with the unfaithful and rather vile Willy. After she left him, she launched into her career as a mime and traveled with a dramatic group throughout France. In *The Vagabond* she writes of this career and also of the marriage she left behind. She discusses the feminine pleasure she found in total devotion (including her suffering) to this man. She even, in ultimate masochism, comforted Willy's abandoned mistresses. She had neither children nor a richness of life with him to tie her to Willy; she was enjoying the purity of her total and monogamous love, an inner ideal that was more important to her than having a satisfactory husband. A kind of virginity is achieved in this total love, an idealism that only the young can embrace even if the object is unworthy. The passion itself is sufficient reward. Chodorow's description of feminine psychology as resting on the tighter, longer pre-Oedipal bonds with the mother probably lies behind the feminine passion to recapitulate that golden age. The passion for an absolute, committed, and containing love destines many women for this all-for-love attitude; it may even be a step toward becoming mothers, becoming that primary parent and first love.

This idealistic attitude toward love and marriage in the young woman may explain why some studies find women more introverted than men in the first half of adult life, (ages 35 to 45). For most women, finding a mate and making a nest are primary goals that can begin in the teens and extend through the early thirties. Many women have to try this in order to find out that it is not for them. Even the most adamantly independent women have often tried to solidify the purity of love in marriage. Germaine Greer comes to mind here. In the early 1970s, newscasts showed her discussing how she was making a habit of pinching men's bottoms on the street and inviting them to her room rather than going to their territory. Yet in 1979, in her mid-thirties and still thrillingly swashbuckling in her independence, she revealed that she had married very briefly in her early twenties, had subsequently wanted to be sterilized (which doctors refused to do because of her age), and now was trying to conceive a child. She told this by way of advising younger women not to make permanent life choices, such as sterilization, before they can be sure of what they want.

Perhaps there is an archetypal feminine dream of a paradise recovered or created in the home of a woman's own making. This is a dream that must be disrupted by reality, sometimes after many years (as with Colette), before a woman can let go of the transpersonal pattern and move on to more individualistic kinds of growth. Some younger women do not live out this literal realization of the grand passion in the institution of marriage, with children, domesticity, and so forth. They merely live with the men. Many live with older men who have teen-aged children. The bitterness and disillusionment that can set into this living arrangement are frightening. These young women understandably resent the intrusion of children into their love lives. The naiveté of the men in thinking that these very young women can become surrogate mothers to teenagers is also remarkable. Yet such women often remain in these relationships for years. There is a kind of built-in unfaithfulness in such relationships, since the biological parent continues to relate to the children and the other parent. The young woman cannot get all of the man's devotion and attention; his children and sometimes his ex-wife distract and detract from the relationship.

As Colette tells us in *The Vagabond*, a woman often embraces the jealousy and pain that an unfaithful husband brings her; she apparently finds the suffering a further proof of her devotion, of which she is very proud. This kind of behavior may be a peculiar and paradoxical form of feminine hubris or pride. If it is not shucked off and rejected, women can spend their whole lives stewing in the juices of their marital pain. If a woman does not make an early break with this kind of marriage or man, her pride in her pain — greater than anyone else's because she has stayed with it — becomes virtually her raison d'être, her excuse for not achieving anything else with her life. (This is generally an aspect of younger women.) One seldom sees a man suffering day by day with the depth and constancy that unhappy wives do. Men tend to discount, forget, and live beyond marital pain. Women can't let it be: they fester in it, form consciousness-raising groups to talk about it.

When women finally make the break, it is often with hair-raising vengeance. Margaret Laurence's *The Diviners* features Morag, who allows her husband to subjugate her into a childish role for nine years. He belittles her writing talents and puts her in her place with such patronizing, seemingly affectionate phrases as "little one." Her harangue about this name is the beginning of her separation from Brooke, a man very much like Colette's Willy:

> "*Little one.* Brooke, I am twenty-eight years old, and I am five feet eight inches tall, which has always seemed too bloody christly tall to me but there it is, and by judas priest and all the sodden saints in fucking Beulah Land, I am stuck with it, and I do not *mind* like I did once, in fact the goddamn reverse if you really want to know, for I've gone against it long enough, and I'm no actress at heart, then, and that's the everlasting christly truth of it."[11]

Morag, like Colette, becomes her true artist-self at the end of her first grand passion.

The grand passion may or may not take the form of marriage for modern women. Yet Erikson sees marriage as central to woman's identity. In his essay "Womanhood and the Inner Space," he asserts that the choice of a marriage partner is central to feminine identity and is parallel to masculine attainment of ego:

> The stage of life crucial for the emergence of an integrated female identity is the step from youth to maturity, the stage when the young woman, whatever her work career, relinquishes the care received from the parental family in order to commit herself to the love of a stranger and to the care to be given to his and her offspring . . . mental and emotional ability to receive and give fidelity marks the conclusion of adolescence.[12]

I would disagree sharply with the significance of Erikson's fifth stage as a boundary. Rather, the *end* of this stage marks the actual birth of the ego in a woman, the transformative rebirth and true beginning of the self's quest in the world. In the past, many women did not live to see this stage through in their own lives. It is important to note that a woman does not need to divorce her husband to extricate herself from the nonindividuating coils of the grand passion. Her growth out of this stage may take the form of a gradually growing friendship with her husband as she lets go of her numinous, godlike images of the masculine, stops projecting them onto him, and accepts him as human. Any woman who remains enveloped in her identity as wife has refused to take the step of growth that fully functioning female adults must. Being a wife is part of many women's identities, including mine, but to exclude other connections to the community may constitute a particular form of women's sin, a concept I develop later. It may be possible for women to individuate solely as homemakers, but it is probably difficult. Laurence's *The Fire Dwellers* shows the difficulty of this even as it portrays its possibility. To attempt such an unlikely feat is unwise, perhaps even a form of selfishness.

When Colette finally leaves Willy, her grand passion, she heals herself by taking Missy, a lesbian lover. It is at this time that her ego and true self-identity are born. She becomes an artist (a writer and a mime) and a lover of women/self. Like Christ, Colette was thirty-three; she entered this new life stage with a crucified ego that was ripened and wise. A woman who enters this life stage brings a thoroughly different ego to her studies, to her new or old career, or to her sojourn into the world of volunteer work. Feminine individuation thus often begins at a time when a man's disgust with the divisive, isolating compulsions of his ego is just beginning. At midlife, when most men begin to seek intimacy, to turn toward a new kind of individuation which, for perhaps the first time in history, our culture is making possible for them, women's egos surface powerfully and in a multifaceted, differentiated form. Colette's significant life work began after her marriage with Willy had ended. Her second marriage, to the brilliant philanderer Henri, ended in divorce too, but it never interrupted her career and life in the way her marriage to Willy did.

Young children can sometimes interrupt and slow down the flow of a young woman's life, yet they often enrich it too. Consider the sculptor Barbara Hepworth, who had a number of children yet casually divorced her first husband, the father of her children. Hepworth's sculpture emphasizes multiple, free-standing feminine forms in tender, intimate, and protective relationship to one another. She says her work was deeply influenced by her experience of pregnancy and mothering; some critics now see her as a major influence on another sculptor, Henry Moore, who also celebrates the feminine principle in his work. The artist Käthe Kollwitz also was deeply inspired by her children. Her enjoyment of them far outweighed the work and difficulty they caused her. The children of an energetic and creative woman generally enhance her life, although despair sometimes arises over the conflict between the children's and the woman's needs.

Even when children are young, each woman should work and read in her chosen life's work. Women who leave the job world completely for ten to twenty-five years and then try to re-enter it are naive about how the system works, their relative place in it, and how much things have changed during the time they have been away. These women often have married wealthy professional men and lived out their own ambitions through their husbands. The lucrative incomes of their husbands have shielded them from much of the arduousness of household management and work and even from some of the rigors of child care, so they have not grown as much as they might have from dealing with these aspects of life. They have also developed an overblown image of their importance through identification with their husbands' jobs. Such magazines as *The Doctor's Wife* carefully define the persona of charitable refinement, the wife as accoutrement, to which these women should reduce themselves; the sense of aristocratic elitism in such magazines is seductive and polished. Too many women fall prey to this kind of role, and enormous amounts of intelligence and energy are wasted in posing for the society section of the local newspaper. Many of these women's egos have remained at an adolescent level of development in terms of lack of commitment or focus, a narcissistic self-evaluation, and concomitant expectations vis-à-vis the job world. Such women tend to become ardent and wrong-headed feminists, imagining that they are not given seniority or the best jobs because they are women. Sometimes, of course, they do encounter prejudice concerning their age or sex, but often the problem lies in the women's failure to understand what they cannot bring to a job because of lack of experience. Women who have stayed abreast of developments in the world outside their home and who have worked at least part-time when their children are young will find life more conflicting, especially in terms of time allotment, but they will be maturing and growing on two important fronts at the same time.

2. Giving Birth
as a Transpersonal Experience

Giving birth is an experience that is available to most women although certainly not universally desired or lived through. But even if a woman does not want to experience it, she can be aware of and appreciate the potential depth of riches it holds. When I first delivered a lecture on giving birth at a conference in 1980, several nuns came to see me afterward. Some cried as they said how much they appreciated someone articulating what they had given up. The tears seemed joyful though the nuns were sad over their sacrifice. A nun who had been raped told me in private about her experience and said that the lecture made her understand why she felt so depressed and desecrated even long after the event. Women in the audience who had given birth and been conscious during the event (many older women had the richness of the experience stolen from them through general anesthesia) also felt that I had helped to name the religious quality of their experience.

In societies that are still untouched by modern technology, women receive more honor and credit for giving birth than do women in our society, probably partially because the experience is more life-risking. In this culture, however, a woman can be made to feel foolish for emphasizing the centrality of giving birth to her identity or her personal religiousness, her "womanspirit."

Two books have attempted to return birth to a sacred position as a religious experience: *Spiritual Midwifery*, by Ina May Gaskin, and *Giving Birth: The Parents' Emotions in Childbirth*, by Sheila Kitzinger. Gaskin and Kitzinger are both midwives, but the books reflect their rather antithetical cultures. Gaskin and many of the members of her commune in Tennessee reflect the 1960s in their drug experiences, and they also integrate Eastern thought into their cosmic spirituality. She sometimes uses words that are incongruous with my experience of birth, such as *rushes* instead of *contractions*. But Gaskin's book is filled with beautiful photographs of birth, babies (including deformed ones, whom this group honors and loves), and fathers as well as mothers. While there is a bothersome sixties dialect, the book is moving and compelling:

> When a child is born, the entire Universe has to shift and make room. Another entity capable of free will, and therefore capable of becoming God, has been born. In that way, every child's birth is exactly like the birth of a world teacher. Every child born is a living Buddha. Some of them only get to be a living Buddha for a moment, because nobody believes it. Nobody knows it, and they get treated like they're dumb. Babies are not dumb. A newborn infant is just as intelligent as you are. When you're relating with him, you should consider that you are relating with a very intelligent being who just doesn't speak your language yet. And you shouldn't do anything gross to him before he learns to speak with you.
>
> The midwife or doctor attending births must be flexible enough to discover the way these laws work and learn how to work within them. Pregnant and birthing mothers are elemental forces, in the same sense that gravity, thunderstorms, earthquakes, and hurricanes are elemental forces. In order to understand the laws of their energy flow, you have to love and respect them for their magnificence at the same time that you study them with the accuracy of a true scientist . . .
>
> Spiritual midwifery recognizes that each and every birth is the birth of the Christ child. The midwife's job is to do her best to bring both the mother and child through their passage alive and well and to see that the sacrament of birth is kept Holy. . . . For [her] touch to carry the power that it must, the midwife must keep herself in a state of grace.[1]

Kitzinger's book, on the other hand, is delightfully British — wry, ironic, reticent. The fathers she discusses are not as receptive to experiencing birth as are the fathers in Gaskin's commune, yet the underlying sacredness that both women find in midwifery is the same.

In addition to these books, the broadest, deepest, and most suggestive data on the maternal metaphysical experience of birth come from the research of Stanislav Grof, head of psychiatric research at Johns Hopkins Medical School. Grof spent the first years of his career in Czechoslovakia, where it is legal for psychiatrists to use psychedelic drugs in therapy. (It is important to note that in both that country and this, doctors who use these drugs insist that they must be used only in controlled clinical settings because they can raise psychoses into consciousness and leave a person permanently devastated. After one LSD session a patient often needs many sessions with a therapist to understand and confront the forces revealed during that first session.) Grof says he first used LSD in his native country in 1955; in 1967 he came to the United States, where he has received grants to work in many well-known research institutes. He has used psychedelic drugs with terminal cancer patients, "hopeless" alcoholics, the insane, convicts with the most illiterate of backgrounds, and, of course, with the middle-class and functionally neurotic. In all cases he has found that patients experience the four stages of birth — oceanic unity with the mother, entrapment in the birth canal as labor begins, the actual birth, and the sense of a new kind of universal bliss after birth. These stages seem to become analogues in later life for extremely intense experiences. A woman trapped in a bad marriage and suffering terrible asthmatic attacks remembered almost choking in a long and difficult birth when the cord wrapped around her neck. The recovered memory allowed her to move out of second-state entrapment and to a psychic rebirth or transformation.

Thus, after a suitable number of LSD sessions, patients "relive" the actual experience of their own births; accompanying the four stages of birth is a mystical and visionary experience, a sort of four-stage transformation that is stimulated by memories of birth. Grof has written several books on the psychological significance of these memories, which he calls perinatal matrices. But one has to delve into his obscure writings to find out what Grof thinks of his research in terms of such metaphysics as ontology or cosmology. In his books he alludes to astrological force fields, memories of previous incarnations, and astral travel, but he concentrates on empirical data that will not alarm his fellow scientists.

Scientists who read Grof prefer to interpret his work from a materialistic point of view. In *Broca's Brain*, Carl Sagan drastically reduces the meaning of Grof's discovery of birth memories to the sole and primary matrix for later memories. Sagan then uses Grof's work to discredit the experiences of visitations and messengers from a spirit world before and during death, so widely written of now. Sagan suggests that death's hormonal release may trigger the memory of birth and that the figures the dying see are actually memories of midwives and obstetricians. This theory does not, however, account for the different figures seen by dying American versus Indian patients. If the godhead or the numinous figures seen by the dying were memories of midwife and obstetrician, then surely Americans would see more male "deities"; but this is not the case. Patients from India experience many more male deities, yet midwifery is widespread there. [2]

Sagan insists that the birth experience is the first and only cause in human personality; that is, personality is based on this first layer of environmental engraving on the psyche. Grof himself does not see the perinatal matrices as a causal nexus but suggests that they bear a formal similarity to something like a Jungian archetype or an elementary cosmic structure. [3] In other words, he sees the possibility that the human psyche is a microcosm that reflects the macrocosm. Perhaps the creative patterns in the universe are like the experience of giving birth; to stretch it further, the Universal Mind/Body (God/Goddess) may experience our deaths in the way our mothers experience our birth. As suggested in Osis and Haraldsson's *At the Hour of Death*, there seems to be a similar delivery system.

In other words, Grof suggests that birth is like some basic cosmological process, and that the human soul experiences this process as it is born or as its body gives birth. When Grof describes the cosmology that seems to be revealed by psychedelic drugs, he suggests that two peak experiences often disclose and connect this universal process to the human mind. One is truly loving sexual relations, especially sexual intercourse that involves all the levels of being, not just the body. The second reflects a unique metaphysical propensity of the feminine psyche, the naming of which may be a landmark in understanding the meaning of gender and the deeper patterns of feminine consciousness. Grof says that a mother can experience giving birth as "a profound unitive experience in which [she] transcend[s] the limits of [her] personality."[4] He strongly emphasizes, however, that a person's attitude can turn sexual union or giving birth into either a transformational experience or a polarizing and negative experience of separation and alienation; the key is that the soul must be receptive to the possibility of transcending its bounds. Of birth he says, "If the mother is emotionally stable and is looking forward to the arrival of the newborn baby, and if the matrimonial situation is harmonious, the delivery can be a very cosmic experience in which the mother transcends herself and experiences this event within a cosmic framework."[5]

This is a whole new emphasis on what the experience of birth can bring. Virtually all other research has concentrated on the importance of a positive birth experience for the infant and for the infant-mother bonding, but little, except for Ina Gaskin's *Spiritual Midwifery*, has focused on the importance of birth for the mother as an individual person, especially in terms of her metaphysical growth. Yet Grof is convinced that a positive birth experience often has deep effects on a woman's religiousness and on her sense of the universe and her place within it.

It is important before going on to a closer analysis of the importance of birth and "mothers' metaphysics" to examine the cosmos that Grof postulates. He says "the most frequently occurring metaphysical problem in psychedelic sessions was that of the existence and nature of a Supreme Being, ultimate force in this Universe, or God."[6] It is intriguing that when subjects saw what we would believe to be embodiments or personifications of Godhead (such as Christ, Isis, or Mary), they did not experience these figures as the Supreme Being. When subjects did encounter the Supreme Being, they experienced no concrete images, which is probably one of the reasons they all agreed that the experience was ineffable. They transcended their usual limitations of self in feeling at one with "infinite existence," "infinite knowledge or wisdom," or "infinite bliss." They also experienced an "ultimate metacosmic and supracosmic nothingness"[7] they called the Void, which had an integral, necessary, and harmonious relationship with the Universal Mind. This is like the Eastern concept of the One and the Many— the One giving birth to the Many, which gradually flow together

back into One, which then gives birth again to the Many, and so on. The Void and the Universal Mind emerge from and disappear into one another, reflecting the primordial, shifting, constant creation of the universe.

The whole cosmos for Grof's patients seems to rest on paradoxes —consistent paradoxes, but suprarational principles nevertheless. Godhead itself, the Universal Mind, is born out of nothingness, a sort of fecund "white hole" which, according to Grof, astrophysicists recently postulated as the antithesis of black holes. (White holes are spaces in which matter appears without any precedent.)

The subjects also discussed the existence of parapsychological phenomena as "deliberate defects in the cosmic screenwork [that] disclose the real nature of the Universe."[8] (Women are more apt to perceive these defects than men are. They are often more aware of the possibilities of telepathic communication than most men are, and can be considered more pious, more receptive listeners to the rhythms of the cosmos. However, they are often branded irrational and superstitious. Some current research even proves that women are more receptive to mystery and the occult, a feminine propensity I discuss later in this book.) Not only are humans the godhead playing hide-and-seek with itself; the cosmos also plays hide-and-seek with us. Out of nothingness (the Void) comes godhead. The womb of nothingness, the white hole, bears the Universal Mind that creates more space, which teems with matter. Many women probably intuit the pattern of birth and rebirth in the cosmos as the potential they themselves embody in their physical beings. The pattern of the cosmos seems thus to be a feminine ground of being.

Woman's body clearly echoes this One-and-Many creation and absorption of godhead. Her dreams show that a woman's unconscious registers her potential to create another being as the menstrual cycle completes itself each month.[9] Whether she chooses to give birth or not, every woman is conscious of the teeming potential of her inner space, her creative void. I am reminded of Erikson's theory of "inner space" (woman's womb as a space either filled or empty) as an innate aspect of woman. This theory enrages some feminists, probably because, like so much of women's imagery, it has been turned against us. Naturally, if one sees the womb as a vacuum, an empty cipher, then one ends up with such

repellent and woman-hating conclusions as those of Jean-Paul Sartre, who said that woman is only a hole desiring to be filled. But this is not how women imagine their wombs. We sense our inner space as a warm, protective, ruby-red, darkly luminous, enfolding place that can contain transformation, that holds all potential. The title of Rita Mae Brown's *Rubyfruit Jungle* suggests the depth and richness of woman's gender consciousness.

Grof stresses the inadequacy of language and the absence of images in his subjects' direct experience of the Universal Mind. Woman's consciousness of birth, its meaning, and its echoes of cosmic patterns is an unconscious, nonimagistic, nonverbal, yet *shared* feminine metaphysic. To be sure, some women have tried to symbolize or flesh out this nonverbal and unconscious metaphysical knowledge. Anaïs Nin's erotica features an unknown female artist who paints flowers that are really vulvas. She "paints a vulva the size of a full-grown woman. At first it looks like petals, the heart of a flower, then one sees the two uneven lips, the fine center line, the wavelike edge of the lips, when they are spread open . . . suggestively vanishing into a tunnel-like repetition, growing from a larger one to a smaller, the shadow of it, as if one were actually entering into it."[10] Judy Chicago has realized Nin's image in her rendition of a plate for Isabella d'Este; this plate pictures a series of chambers receding infinitely into one another as Isabella's feminine essence. The rubyfruit image of Rita Mae Brown is echoed in Chicago's plates for Margaret Sanger and Susan B. Anthony— glorious blood-red, flaming, vulva-shaped banners of triumph.

The creation of others by the Universal Mind also reflects some imagery natural to women. Grof's patients' Universal Mind became lonely and suffered from monotony and boredom which resulted in "diffuse craving for change and partnership";[11] then creation began through a partitioning away from godhead. Perhaps the current interest in "roots," or past generations, is part of a sacred urge to find godhead through tracing oneself back through one's origins. Grof says, however, that while each creature is part of the Universal Mind, partitioning results in forgetfulness and loss of the source, which is finally even violently denied. It is at this point that "a radical qualitative transformation is necessary for a temporary restoration of the original unity."[12] This is like Maslow's idea of peak experiences that keep the person going and faithful to meaning

even during the doldrums of everyday life that come between the peaks. Grof's peak experiences are, however, more profoundly religious and even mystical.

For men, the major means of reuniting with the source of being seems to be the male-female fusion, which in its highest form can give a sense of mystical union. Perhaps the male emphasis on sexuality is part of a metaphysical urge which for men has had only one major avenue.[13] It is possible, however, that as men begin to share in the experience of their children's birth, and if they identify enough with the mothers of their children, they too may experience the transformative qualities of birth. For example, in *The Dispossessed*, Ursula Le Guin's protagonist, Shevek, lives in a world where the birthing experience is part of his motivation to keep his family together. Shevek participates in the birth of his child and watches over his wife and newborn infant after the midwife leaves: "The baby and Takver were already asleep. Shevek put his head down near Takver's . . . Very gently he put one arm over her as she lay on her side with the baby against her breast. In the room heavy with life he slept."[14]

Although his culture teaches this as "propertarian egoizing" (Le Guin's term), Shevek always returns to his partner and children. Perhaps men can learn to value children as deeply as women do, and for the same reasons, if they witness birth. I recently heard a father say that participating in the birth of his child was the most significant event of his life. It may be that part of the mysterious bonding that the medical profession now recognizes as integral to mothers and infants is actually a metaphysical moment when both parents experience the sacred process of producing a new individual. The parents, and perhaps the infant, too, recognize the transpersonal importance of family unity as the creative microcosm. Out of the parental dyad comes a new One. The family is the gate and supporting system for the creation of new life. In fact, how much has modern technology in hospitals interrupted family bonding and contributed to the dissolution of family ties? Experiencing birth together may be a major way of enhancing and giving meaning to family bonds.

If a woman is open to the deep religious values inherent in the process of her body, then another aspect of the birth experience that Grof uncovered becomes enormously significant. Sometimes Grof's female patients were not sure if they were re-experiencing their own births or their children's, which suggests that to give birth is to relive one's own birth from a wider point of view. One can see why the Lamaze and LaBoyer systems (which emphasize bonding and full parental control and participation) have the long-term effects of more positive family relationships and healthier, happier children. Not only is the infant's birth trauma softened, but the mother's own personal birth trauma is broadened and relayered in a positive and conscious way. A friend of mine wrote about her own pregnancy by recalling a dream she had:

> I was in the hospital giving birth. It was wonderful — so easy and gentle. After the baby was born, quietly, calmly, she/he sat up and smiled. I was flooded with happiness. I was leaving the birthing room and I saw *myself* being pushed into the labor room, crying and screaming wildly because the birth was going to be everything I didn't want it to be, medicated, forceps, etc. I felt so betrayed. The interesting part, though, is this self I was looking at was in a newborn's isolette — so "I" appeared to be both mother and baby. At first I took the dream to be about how much I wanted to be in control of the birth of this baby — but now I see it was about my own birth. My mother, as was typical for the time, was completely unconscious during delivery. This was during World War II. When I was six months old, she left me with my grandmother until I was a year old. An oft-told story was how she left a skinny little black-haired baby and came home to a chubby, golden-haired one. The story was always part of the "family romance." My father was in the Navy . . . living conditions were impossible for a baby — it was so cold in Maine — she had to be with my father, he might never come back, etc. I always accepted this story with great equanimity until I had Anne — and then I was flooded with feelings best expressed as "How could she . . . ?" Of course, I've often had to say that about the quality of mothering I've given. I think the dream was one of a promise of reconciliation, of the establishment of a bond of near-perfect love as both child and mother.

This dream and my friend's interpretation of it made me wonder about some of the basic patterns of the feminine psyche. Women have not consciously understood the meaning that childbearing can hold; this meaning probably resides at a deep level, even if a woman's conscious self does not acknowledge it. I used to dream of giving birth to tiny infants, about six inches long, who were in grave danger from masked doctors who brandished sharp and shiny chrome instruments as they tore around the delivery room. How much is this a reliving of my own birth, which was like my friend's, and my eldest daughter's birth (when I was twenty) which was as brutal and dehumanizing as modern technology could make it? I had another child in my late thirties — a good birth during which I was conscious, my husband present, the child immediately given to me. The memories of this birth are exceedingly comforting, and I cannot remember having the dreams of mutilation since then. This suggests that the desire to have a child may be a very deep metaphysical urge toward reconciliation and harmony.

Pregnancy also can be a mystical experience of being at one with an essential other. Grof found that many patients knew while still in the womb whether their mothers wanted them, if their mothers were happy, and so on. Probably it is difficult to experience the individuality of the fetus during a first pregnancy, but during later pregnancies many mothers know through fetal movement, rhythms, and sometimes a kind of telepathy,[15] what sort of a person they are going to give birth to. Women have been forced to repress this knowledge by a culture that in its masculine orientation prefers to see pregnancy as purely physical and mechanistic; yet women often speak of these things to each other. Women sometimes suffer from a sense of emptiness after birth, and this is undoubtedly more than physiological; the ease of the closest relationship is complicated by the infant's arrival in the world.

Woman's deep spiritual connections to and reverence for her body make clear why a woman undergoes such deep repugnance and existential nausea when she suffers rape or incestuous abuse. A modern depth psychologist, James Hillman, says that rape is a forcing together of two ontologically different realms; to a woman, her body is literally a temple that reflects or even *is* sacred process, and to suffer rape is an assault on her metaphysics. Women never fully recover from rape and often brood over it all their lives. Men find this inability of women to simply forget an experience of rape puzzling; a modern male writer guesses that rape is simply being out of control and fearful for one's life for half an hour.[16] The experience of rape is a terrible knowledge of nihilism that can never be truly understood or accepted as a part of life.

According to recent studies on the terrible violence that exists between male homosexuals, sadism has been found to be a masculine pathology; mutilating attacks are not a feminine mode of pathology. Women tend to sin through passivity, through not asserting or defining self. It may be impossible for women to ever understand why men rape. When one looks at such phenomena as rape, it is hard not to see the two human sexes as very separate species. One wonders, too, whether some men are angry in the depths of their souls over women's access to the creative processes of life and birth. The Nazis, certainly in the grip of a demonic rebirth fantasy, particularly assaulted, tortured, and killed infants and pregnant women in the death camps; it was as though they wanted to take back, to devour and internalize, special feminine knowledge and experience.

We do not know yet what desires or fantasies underlie the crime of rape, but it probably has to do with a masculine rage and alienation that goes far beyond the family background or relationships of the criminal. When the transcendent possibility of sexual union is understood, rape seems a form of masculine self-annihilation. It is interesting to note here that a recent book investigating the psychological profile of rapists says that inability to ejaculate is one of the two most common problems of rapists, while in non-offenders only one man out of seven hundred has this problem.[17] This physical symptom suggests fear of sexual union itself, fear of women, the desire to withhold self from others; thus the rapist may be suffering from great metaphysical loneliness. When rape is finally understood, we may have our finger on the specific metaphysical problems that men suffer. Rape from the woman's point of view, however, is a terrible desecration and denial both of her holy potential to give birth and of sexual union as a spiritual and mystical peak.

A concept which Grof feels possibly further explains women's sacred sense of giving birth is reincarnation; he feels that some of the material recovered by subjects in LSD sessions can only be explained in terms of previous incarnations. If the reincarnation theory of the human soul is valid, then women's experience of birth becomes even more broadly significant. If the soul is immortal, then to die is surely the purest form of birth. And if the soul is reborn many times, then the experience of birth is a death of the infant's previous soul-consciousness yet a birth into a new incarnation. Again, the pattern of birth seems to echo the hide-and-seek pattern of the Universal Mind, a pattern which Grof calls the cosmic game. Thus woman may derive primal knowledge about death from the experience of birth; this knowledge could be the deepest and most ecstatic affirmation of universal patterns possible at this level of existence.

Joan Grant, who has written widely on the religious beliefs of reincarnationists and also on her own "far memory" of previous lives, says that in the Egyptian temples, a priest or priestess had to recover the memory of at least ten deaths from previous lives in order to minister to the dying and truly reassure them. Grant says that as a child during the First World War, she left her body during dreams to assist dying soldiers in their acceptance of their new realm of being. Like Elisabeth Kübler-Ross, Joan Grant was a nurse to dying victims of war. And like Kübler-Ross, Grant sees herself as appointed by higher forces and previous life experiences to the task of assisting the dying in their transition. I think it is not an accident that both these people are female.

The point is that women's bodies are far more reflective than men's of the universal process which may be in fact God's mind and body. We all remember the insistence of certain Christian traditions that Adam was the perfect copy of God and that Eve, because of her reproductive abilities, was an imperfect and distorted copy. In *Paradise Lost*, John Milton has Adam decry God's excessive attention to Eve's outer charms and attractions which kept Him from making her mind and soul as exact and pure as a man's. In reality, the opposite may be true: that man is the more alienated creature of our species. Woman's body is more the temple and reflection of the process of creation. Even the waxing and waning of menstrual energy is an example of the hide-and-seek process, the inevitable coming and going of life.

Grof and his coworkers note that Americans have trouble accepting the mystical consciousness that comes with what some perceive as the unearned and therefore undeserved psychedelic mystical experience.[18] Woman's experience of creation through her body is such an unearned experience — she does not pray or study for it. Yet, as with the LSD subjects, the hardest work comes after a woman has lived out the experience, when she must integrate her insights into her ongoing life as "an unfolding process of renewal" that results in a deeper involvement in the world. Some studies suggest, strikingly, that the more committed women are to their families and children, the stronger and healthier they are as older women. This does not deny that many patterns other than specifically feminine ones are necessary for women's individuation. But many women see the experience of birth as mystical, something they turn over and refocus on all their lives. The more deeply women have lived out the patterns that the body affords them, the more they will "generally feel thrown back into the very heart of life in this world and feel also that they have been given the inner strength to cope with suffering and struggle in society."[19]

The neo-Freudians call this eros aspect of the feminine psyche simply a reflection of woman's strong and lengthy pre-Oedipal ties with the mother. Yet most women desire intercourse with men. There is the archetypal wish to act out the "royal couple." The ancient alchemists imaged the basic chemical element as the royal couple, a crowned lion and lioness standing on their hind legs. June Singer's book *Androgyny* is a celebration of this great archetype of polarity and its fusion into one. She sees it as the duality that encompasses all others.

To love and connect is a natural, cosmic, innate pattern or life urge in our species, just as to experience their potential fecundity concretely is part of most women's life urge. Even in the most crippling circumstances, this urge toward eros, toward connection, can usually still be discerned. Consider the behavioral psychologist B. F. Skinner. His theory of positive reinforcement is just a scientific label for giving love. His methods work with normal human beings only insofar as there actually *is* love within the giver of the positive reinforcements. If the person who receives these tokens discerns that the approach is mechanical, manipulative, or meaningless, he or she quickly loses interest. Skinner's motivation of love can also be seen in his complete and rather vehement rejection of punishment. His idea of utopia is to set up a painless society which brings about growth only through positive reinforcement. This is surely an example of great *eros*; love is playing at hide-and-seek even when love is not an allowable term.

Women's metaphysics as reflected in the meaning of birth is beginning to surface even in some male-generated theology. Process theology, for example, introduces into Christianity a concept of the universe and of godhead that is not unlike the mother body: "The receptive, empathetic, suffering, redemptive, preservative aspect of God . . . that in Whitehead's vision is the 'feminine' aspect of God that is final, inclusive, and fully actual."[20] In other words, the loving, containing, embracing quality of the universe is more real to process theologians than the more traditional qualities of the Logos God: "Order, novelty, call, demand, agent, transformer, and the principle of restlessness."[21] Thus many men have always believed in a feminine godhead but not known it.

Part of woman's religious urge to experience the potential of her body is caught for me in the phrase "transcending downward," a phrase coined by Kenneth Burke.[22] The term means a good deal more to me than Burke, however; I think of psyche renewing and discovering itself by touching, diving into, and being surrounded by the ground of being, matter–nature–mother. The maternal identification with the infant is a direct link to the uroboric beginnings of consciousness. Margaret Atwood's novel *Surfacing* is a splendid demonstration of a woman giving birth to herself, transcending downwards. Women's own body, not only nature, is an available ground of being that is in this way fuller than the masculine sense of body seems to be. A woman's body is rooted to cosmic reality in a way the male body is not. This is probably why the decision as to whether to have a child is so much more painful and protracted for a woman than for a man. A woman has a lot more to lose; to have a child is a much more significant experience for her. Reflective of second thoughts in this matter is the fact that the birthrate among women over thirty is the only birthrate rising in the U.S. today. This shows that women who have spent the first stage of their adult lives individuating in hitherto masculine modes, developing their intellect and talents in the larger context of society, in short, transcending upward, are not afraid to reach back and complete their feminine selfhood, to transcend downward. For woman down is up. These older mothers will probably experience birth more deeply than younger mothers and will be more open about sharing its meaning in the years to come.

One radical application of the importance of birth in woman's metaphysics is the absolute and urgent need for female clergy, including women who have given birth. I was raised a Christian and once in a while still attend a Christian church. I have always experienced myself as an alien in that tradition, but in the past few years I have begun to see that my puzzlement over and sense of estrangement from the church has come from my perception of the trinity as a divine male bonding. I have always distantly admired Christ as a sort of brother, and though he is the most spiritual brother I could imagine, he is still not in touch with the essence of divinity that I have experienced. When I was in my early twenties, one of my daughters died, and I found masculine clergy, even if they were fathers, absolutely unhelpful. In fact, sometimes they aggravated the grief. Other women, especially older ones who were also mothers, were much more able to connect with my pain and help me to understand it. But like should be able to turn to like *within* the body of any church, and women's point of view should be given official status so that it can be more easily sought and found.

For hundreds of years, women have been denigrated so completely that they have not thought their knowledge special enough to bring to the level of consciousness. In the last hundred years, waves of feminism have occurred as women have copied male individuation as a way to fuller personhood. Now, there is a new movement of women trying to find out who in fact we really are. Woman is giving birth to herself—an awesome cataclysm. As Margaret Laurence, one of my favorite authors, says in a new application of her Scottish forebears' motto, "Gainsay who dares." Woman is coming out of hiding and bringing her secrets with her.

3. The Nursing Mother and Feminine Metaphysics

Not all women are mothers and not all mothers breast-feed, of course; but if a woman does nurse her baby, she can experience mystical and even metaphysical levels of her soul. If she is receptive to the knowledge that her body offers her, she can experience a revelation that has its own special grace.

It is well known that breast-feeding has advantages for the infant and for the mother-infant bonding. It has also been established that women are rewarded for lactation in terms of their own health, and perhaps even erotically. I want to address the significance of breast-feeding as an aspect of women's religiousness, part of a feminine theology that women have lived without writing or speaking of it, keeping instead that feminine silence that is so ancient, deep, and fraught with knowledge.

UNITY, CONTAINMENT, AND TRANSCENDING DOWNWARD

There is nothing like the monumental statis of the filled, often dozing baby and the relief of the previously taut breast; being and becoming merge in a concrete way. As the mother lets go of her ego, identifying instead with the baby's satisfaction, she may feel a sense of total unity with the child that is not unlike the more mystical moments of pregnancy. The gradual relaxation of the infant and mother until they have almost merged during a feeding is a form of *mysterium conjunctio*, both psychic and physical unification. Not only women have recognized this phenomenon; certain Renaissance artists who were particularly enamored of the feminine principle often painted Mary and the Christ Child tranquil and serene together after a nursing.

A nursing mother's sense of immersion in the body, the feeling of transcending downward through lactation, may even in fact be the most complete physical experience available to woman. The experience of nursing contains the mother and sets her apart not only from surrounding persons but from within, through her own body consciousness. Because tissue from the breast spreads around a woman's body, into her sides below the arms, the sensation of nursing surrounds the female body. Some women even sense the milk as being drawn from their backs, though the tissue is not there. This gives them a larger, more total sense of flowing out of self.

The flowing of the milk can be a holistic bodily metaphor for maternal *caritas*, an open, nurturing world love. Lactation may even provide the basis, the psychological ground, for future maternal feelings; a mother may relive her bodily response of joy as her child receives fulfillment from other life experiences. Women who force their children to eat, who stuff them with food instead of love, may be extending their lactation powers and fulfillment, forcing the children to act as replete and filled vessels of their gift of nourishment. This sort of mother may need weaning herself. Like everything, delight in the child as container can become pathological, but in normal proportions, maternal pride and joy in the child's feeding (its "containing" of maternal love) underlie an unselfish delight in the child's unique growth.

> Her future feeling for the child, when this close postpartum tie has been outgrown and it is a rambunctious toddler (indeed even later, when it is a pimply adolescent, or a greying eccentric), will always be flavored on some level—as it could not for a less intelligent mammal—with the memory of the passion which at this moment knots her belly and makes her nipples spurt.[1]

When I look at my oldest daughter, now twenty-five, I feel the oddest metaphysical start or shock to realize that this adult person is the same burrowing, suckling creature (the image of lovable larva comes to my mind) I nursed so many years ago. This gives me a special tenderness toward all adults, as I can psychically unpeel the layers of maturity and see the needy and vulnerable infant that all of the adult unfolding builds from and covers over. Perhaps women, through caring for infants and especially through the very concrete act of nursing, have a sense of the primordial seed in each person and of the mystery of human development which is often harder for men to come by.

MOTHER-INFANT SENSE OF REALITY

Physiological interaction between child and mother during the actual act of suckling clearly deepens their bond and their knowledge of each other. The infant learns to make the milk come; it learns patience with the irregularity of the flow of milk and of mother love itself, which in most cases is constant but inconsistent and varied. The bottle, in fact, seems an unfair image of biological or maternal reality for the infant; the bottle is always the same, and life is not like that. The mother's moods change her flow, and her diet changes the milk itself. The mother's body, both before and after birth, is the primary and first experience of the world for all infants. The occasional supplementary bottle can be viewed within this context as a lesson in the difference between mother and others and also as an assurance that the world contains caring others.

The mother's nursing body also helps her learn to understand her child. The mother's whole body, not just her hearing, learns which tenor of cry is the hunger call; her milk surges forward or drops involuntarily as she awakens to the call at night. A mother learns to associate the infant's hunger with her own relief. Any sensitive and attentive mother also learns the differences among her infants' personalities through the way they feed and respond to her milk flow. One may be an intense and concentrating infant who grabs hold of the nipple and never slacks off until it is full; another may stop feeding to smile at its mother occasionally. Bottle-fed babies may do the same, but many infants fondle the breast or pat it playfully as they become older, and this may even presage the special affection the older child will give to the mother.

GRACE, GODHEAD, AND NURSING

Helpful to a larger understanding of breast-feeding is Judith Plaskow's analysis of Tillich and Niebuhr, who define religion from the point of view of masculine spirituality. In their theologies, all sin is relegated to the trait of pride; Niebuhr furthermore connects pride and human "creatureliness," which he distrusts. Plaskow convincingly argues that women's central sin involves the opposite of pride, "the failure to take responsibility for becoming a self,"[2] a sin which Tillich sidesteps but calls "uncreative weakness."[3] Plaskow also takes Niebuhr (and Simone de Beauvoir) to task for their attitudes toward woman's connection with nature, arguing that "care and socialization of children [are] viewed as natural functions; they could be seen as cultural processes of the highest order."[4] Levi-Strauss classifies nature and culture as "the raw and the cooked." Women cooking, women gestating, women nursing are all images of nature being converted to culture. Woman's body is a transmutation system; it has the power to change blood to milk, to change itself to food which in turn becomes the physical and psychic energy of a child. She is creating an incarnate soul, assisting it in growth.

Furthermore, a woman can gain a specifically feminine sense of grace during breast-feeding, a form of what Tillich calls revelation. But one must be open to and accepting of grace. It must become culturally permissible to find value, all kinds of value, in knowledge that comes through the body. In other words, woman may be making or finding self and soul through her body, through nature. Woman perhaps moves through nature as lived out in a finite body, in order to clarify the meaning of self while man moves against nature. For woman, nature and culture are not as sharply different as for man.

Woman's milk can be seen as a kind of *agape* (a spiritual love that mingles nature and grace) that materializes to flow through the child and thence into the universe. Tillich sees grace as reconstitution of the self which manifests through participation and interaction with others. Nursing can be among the deepest forms of communion, affording a grace that comes through an effortless participation and giving—a bonus, perhaps, for the often crushing arduousness of other facets of mothering, such as tending to indefatigable infants who are teething. The bluish, thin, translucent human milk even has a spiritual appearance. The way that one breast can leak while an infant suckles the other suggests an oddly communal quality even between the breasts, perhaps "sisters in charity." I am a thin and small-breasted woman and have always felt awe at this obvious surplus, a surfeit of nature with implications for the plenitude that the image of Goddess embodies.

The knowledge gained from breast-feeding is not a passing one, but a reference point in the consciousness of many women for their whole lives. Anne Sexton's poetry demonstrates the primal and permanent qualities of this knowledge. In her last poetic affirmation of life, the nine "Psalms" which conclude *The Death Notebooks*, Anne Sexton portrays milk as feminine and cosmic grace. An earlier reference in the book foreshadows the strength of the symbol of milk as transcendent and celebratory. Sexton imagines a dream mother: "At the cup of her breasts/ I drew wine,"[5] an image which suggests the Holy Grail or the cup of communion. The earlier sections of the book also feature the symbol of a dead baby, which juxtaposes with and deepens the later exaltation in the "Seventh Psalm":

> For the baby suckles and there is a people made of milk for her to use.
> There are milk trees to hiss her on. There are milk beds in which to lie and dream of a warm room. There are milk fingers to fold and unfold. There are milk bottoms that are wet and caressed and put into their cotton.
> For there are many worlds of milk to walk through under the moon.[6]

In the last five lines of the final "Ninth Psalm," Sexton blesses with milk her personal icon of human misery—the rat, her shadow brother Christopher, and herself:

> For they hung up a picture of a rat and the rat smiled and held out his hand.
> For the rat was blessed on that mountain. He was given a white bath.
> For the milk in the skies sank down upon them and tucked them in.[7]

The Death Notebooks thus ends in celebration of milk as the connective tissue, the flow, the indisputable plenitude of a loving ground of being. In her later poetry, Sexton unfortunately seeks connections with a masculine god; she no longer projects her own feminine images into a vision of a patterned, containing and loving universe. This, I believe, is part of what precipitated her suicide.

As James Hillman explains in *The Myth of Analysis*, the human body is the basic image in all philosophy.[8] Women need to envision godhead from their own bodies' experience, not from masculine perceptions. Men who learn of how woman's body reflects and projects images of godhead will see that their own ideas are one-sided, though valid for them. Men will find there is another perspective or godhead that will perhaps afford them welcome relief from some of the more negative manifestations of masculine godhead.

Sexton's imagery is not unique to her but has a history. Both classical and Christian references use milk as a cosmic metaphor. Since these ideas probably came from men, we can see that intuitive, sensitive men (often breast-fed as infants, after all) did understand some of the spiritual meanings of breast-feeding. The Romans connected milk with "the eternity of the heavens": "For on one night Juno's milk, when she was nursing Hercules, sprayed across the sky and created the Milky Way, our galaxy. The Greek *galaktos* means milk; *lac*, the Latin for milk, derives from the same root."[9] The seventh-century theologian Bede also reflects this cosmology when he speaks of the Virgin's milk: "Thou whose blessed breasts, filled with a gift from on high, fed for all lands the unique glory of earth and heaven."[10] As Marina Warner remarks, "The highest life was expressed by the milk of a mother—white, gleaming, and moist, a pure equivalent of light."[11]

THE NURSING POET

The sense of ebb and flow, cyclical fullness, self as literal vessel, container, or conduit, often lends a contemplative mode to the act of nursing, which connects a woman's roots with the earth and its dark, profound mysteries, especially at night. Apart from the rest of her family, who sleep, the mother feels herself and her baby at the quiet center of the universe. Through no deliberate act or volition, nature creates and flows through her ("gratuitous grace"); she is the giver of the primordial life-stuff, the builder of human flesh, her milk more than any other substance made to emanate human life. There is a kind of vegetative principle working through her that gives her insight into nature on a direct and bodily level.

A few women have written of this experience. Sylvia Plath begins her book *Ariel* with a poem set in the stillness of a night nursing, a peculiarly feminine stasis.

MORNING SONG

Love set you going like a fat gold watch.
The midwife slapped your footsoles and your bald cry
Took its place among the elements.

Our voices echo, magnifying your arrival. New statue.
In a drafty museum, your nakedness
Shadows our safety. We stand round blankly as walls.

I'm no more your mother
Than the cloud that distils a mirror to reflect its own slow
Effacement at the wind's hand.

All night your moth-breath
Flickers among the flat pink roses. I wake to listen:
A far sea moves in my ear.

One cry, and I stumble from bed, cow-heavy and floral
In my Victorian nightgown.
Your mouth opens clean as a cat's. The window square

Whitens and swallows its dull stars. And now you try
Your handful of notes;
The clear vowels rise like balloons.[12]

For the first three and a half stanzas, she considers the miracle of mothering a child who is essentially a stranger but who arrives through her body. She has awakened before the cry, as many mothers do, sensing the hunger of the infant. The infant then pulls her into the world of giving, which though biological in essence (she is heavy as a cow with milk, and her child takes the breast like a cat), is also a mysterious, spiritual, and cosmic principle of creation. The child's swallowing is compared with the morning light's swallowing stars, and its replete delight rises, a sort of music, transcendant and festive in the air. This unique poem depicts one of the secrets of womankind, the joy and mystery of night nursing.

Some male writers have also sensed the contemplative and lyrical qualities of the nursing mother and child. In Herman Melville's *Moby Dick*, the feminine world is rendered in an image of the male characters gazing into the depths of the ocean at a group of female whales giving birth to and suckling their young. But while men can often appreciate the image of mother-and-infant bliss, only female artists such as Sylvia Plath have been able to share the subjective experience of this archetype.

Throughout history, male writers and thinkers have actively defined lactation. Part of reclaiming the female body (remembering what it means) is to study and peel off masculine fantasies that have become unconscious and contaminate women's sense of their bodies. Up until the fifteenth century the Virgin's milk was seen as infinite, an image of grace available to all humans. After that time, lactation was emphasized as part of woman's biological humiliation, brought on by the Fall. As a result, wet-nursing became widespread in western culture.[13] Warner sees this rejection of nursing as part of the Reformation and the spread of puritanism.[14] In our own time, bottle-feeding is the continuation of this negative assessment of nursing. Some of the early Christians saw Mary's milk as having an intermediary quality. The image of Mary standing between God the punishing father and Christ and/or sinners, offering up her breast or drops of milk to protect them, probably reflects male Oedipal fantasies.

Some male writers have also projected fearful and negative images of lactation, even mingling mutilation and the tearing apart of infants with the act of suckling. The Dionysian Maenads in Euripides' *The Bacchae* dismember humans and animals, yet they force the mother earth to suckle them:

. . . Those who desired
Milk had only to scratch the earth with finger-tips,
And there was the white stream flowing for them to drink.[15]

They also nurse Zoë (life force), which appears in the form of a wolf cub or gazelle. These images reflect a masculine fear of breast-feeding; the imagery of animals, mutilation, and women regressing into suckling infants denies the spirituality and the essential and personal love that the nursing mother imparts.

Yet despite these negative connotations, milk has symbolized the essence of mother love. A brief etymological reverie will show the cross-cultural acknowledgment of this, for the word clusters surrounding the idea of nursing are positive. The word *mammal* comes from the Latin *mamma*, which means "breast." *Webster's New World Dictionary* links *mama* with a hypothetical Indo-European *mandama*, which means "to suck, breast," "to be moist, damp," "to flow."

In Anne Sexton's vision of grace, milk flows and moistens the universe, so that the poet unifies and consoles all creatures with mother love or milk. Her imagery is not violent or mutilating. It aligns itself with the Christian conception of milk and honey. Women seem to separate their sense of pain or metaphysical anguish from lactation, which creates a connective oneness with nature. Although Sexton and Plath both finally killed themselves, their earlier and most positive images related to aspects of mothering.

Other women writers also write of breast-feeding from a positive point of view. In Toni Morrison's *Song of Solomon*, Ruth, a deprived and miserable woman, finds nursing her last baby her sole pleasure in life: "She had the distinct impression that his lips were pulling from her a thread of light. It was as if she were a cauldron issuing spinning gold. Like the miller's daughter — the one who sat at night in a straw-filled room, thrilled with the secret power Rumplestiltskin had given her: to see golden thread stream from her very own shuttle."[16] This passage reflects the power and worth that women feel they magically produce. Weaving light or gold within a secret dark room is an image that one often finds in women's descriptions of themselves as artists. Mary Daly, a feminist theologian, and the poet Adrienne Rich both connect spinning and weaving with the most spiritual manifestation of the feminine principle. So Morrison's Ruth perhaps experiences nursing as the expression of herself as artist, magician, alchemist, priestess.

SOME PERSONAL REFLECTIONS

Recently a close friend, Ann, who had been hit by a series of disasters, received a call from her friend Jacquie. Jacquie, a medium who "hears" and interprets messages from the spirit world, had received a message from her spirits that Ann needed a special psychic healing before Jacquie left town on a business trip. After they had meditated together and Jacquie had conferred special energy transmissions, she told Ann, "When I feel that someone needs healing, the divine energy flows up into the heart and breast area. I can only describe this as like being at a party three miles away when your breasts fill and you know the baby's hungry. The urgency to get home and feed it is like wanting to heal someone who needs it." Ann was nurtured and healed by Jacquie's love, and Jacquie experienced the desire to give that loving energy in an especially feminine way — like nursing at a spiritual level. Both women felt relief and serenity, one from the release of pent-up love and the other from its flow surrounding her, a kind of feminine grace.

Teachers of kundalini yoga have always taught that the heart is the center that receives and gives cosmic love. The energy wells up from the libidinal *chakra* (yogic term for spiritual centers) at the bottom of the spine and is transmuted into a feeling of overwhelming love in the heart *chakra*. Other mammals have their nursing apparatus much lower, near the sexual *chakra*, while the primates' and humans' are higher, perhaps denoting a higher form of maternal love. Women's breasts and adjacent tissue surround the heart *chakra*, perhaps one of the reasons that full breasts symbolize spiritual as well as erotic and maternal love in some religious traditions. In her lyrical book *The Moon and the Virgin*, Nor Hall points out that in Greek tradition the first winecup was designed in the shape of the breasts of Helen of Troy; this echoes the quality of spiritual communion that the ancients recognized in women's breasts.

In the Renaissance, the Christian triad of hope, faith, and charity prevailed, but the central virtue from which all others flowed was thought to be charity. Charity was usually depicted as a nursing mother, sometimes with a whole litter of suckling infants. In Spenser's *The Faerie Queene*, the Redcrosse Knight comes to the place of spiritual rehabilitation and is led into Charity's inner sanctum, since she is too busy with her children to greet him as do Faith and Hope. Charity is described this way:

> She was a woman in her freshest age,
> Of wondrous beauty, and of bountie rare,
> With goodly grace and comely personage, . . .
> Her necke and breasts were ever open bare,
> That ay thereof her babes might sucke their fill;
> The rest was all in yellow robes arayéd still . . .
>
> A multitude of babes about her hong,
> Playing their sports, that joyed her to behold,
> Whom still she fed, whiles they were weake and young,
> But thrust them forth still, as they wexéd olde . . .[17]

Charity is in charge of the House of Penance, where the Redcrosse Knight learns all the acts of mercy and love, such as caring for widows and orphans.

One orphan that I learned to care about was a mongoloid infant. When nursing my last child, I was asked by a foster mother, a friend of mine, to nurse this infant who had been given up at birth by his mother. The baby was allergic to formula and needed breast milk to heal his very raw diaper rash. Nursing this little boy was gratifying and fulfilling in a different way from nursing my own children; the impersonal *caritas* of giving to this waif put me in touch with a new aspect of the goddess Demeter, the nurse who gives to the needy infant and then passes on her way.

This experience (six years ago) has had a remarkable effect on my fantasy life. When I feel especially joyful and loving toward the world, the memory of that infant sometimes comes to me, not as a visual image, but as a tactile image. I feel him in my arms and smell his aroma; sometimes I even sense the milk dropping. He remains more vivid to me than my own children at the same age. The experience reminds me of the seventeenth-century Catholic depiction of the Virgin Mary standing in heaven and streaming milk as divine grace down onto the world. While such a portrait seems banal and even grotesque to me, a disinterested giving of milk seems apt to describe one way in which women experience the giving of love.

During the same time I was nursing that infant, another aspect of nursing revealed itself to me. I was teaching full-time during the infancies of my last two children but managed to juggle my schedule so I could breast-feed them for some time. My daughter weaned herself at five months, and I weaned my son at fourteen months. My own anxiety, even anguish, during their first three years of life makes me believe that separation from a small child for more than four or five hours is an unnatural and painful experience for a mother. The psychic longing for both of them was sometimes unbearable. The accumulation of breast-milk and the pent-up desire for them peculiarly echoed each other. This longing and the relief at being with my children again (each would immediately want to suckle, even if she or he had just had a supplementary bottle) constitute some of the deepest passions I have experienced. The older the child, the less acute that longing; but it is a commingling of psyche and body in feminine yearning and love that is highly specific to the mother-child bond.

Breastfeeding, then, as well as other biological functions, connects women to a special kind of wisdom. Rather than separating woman from the spiritual realm, nature actually connects her more surely to cosmic principles, giving her direct access to metaphysical knowledge. As Marguerite Duras says,

> Men are what they are, that is invalids of nature, because they do not have the possibility of experiencing anything like motherhood . . .

women tell themselves that it is because they wipe their children, are buried, submerged by this inevitable concreteness that women are not philosophers. But how false, how childish that is. When you think or say that, your criterion becomes masculine: you think philosophy is the spoken (or written) expression of philosophy, that the concept, likewise, is the articulation of the concept. *I think there is more generality in women than in men and that the "concept" is lived more by the feminine than by the masculine . . . We must move on to the rhetoric of women, one that is anchored in the organism, in the body.*[18]

Some men, such as the sculptor Henry Moore or Leonardo da Vinci, have used woman's body to symbolize the transmutation of the physical world into culture and spirit; but women *live* this process. It is important to human religion that women write and speak of their bodily experiences. Through women the body will once again become sacred as a conduit of grace and spiritual knowledge. The Western polarization of the body and the soul can be softened and modified, as women teach our species of the transformations possible through transcending downward. Even when women pass beyond this stage of life, the years of mothering, most women remember all their lives the lessons of universal process that their bodies have taught them. Feminine metaphysics takes as its bedrock a knowledge gleaned from women's concrete deep-rootedness in the ground of being, which the female body at least equally well expresses and experiences as the so-called superior and more authentic copies of God, Adam, and his sons. The collective unconscious of women carries sacred images not available to men; and women understand from the depths of their unconscious that process, not absolutes, *is* Being.

4. The Older Woman as Matriarch

Men have many established images of patriarchs to choose among for role models as they grow into old age. The Wise Old Man who appeared in C. G. Jung's dreams and waking visions, for example, is a majestic forerunner of Jung's own fruitful and fulfilled old age. Christians have the image of God the Father; one only needs to think of the Sistine Chapel to see the power and creativity that this image promises older men. The ancient Greeks and Romans glorified the older man; the names of their ruling councils, the *gerousia* and the *senatus*, come from the words *geron* and *senex*, meaning "old man." Both cultures featured examples of the wise, creative old politician, such as Cicero. In Greek myth, Teresias gained wisdom in old age from his earlier experience of having been transformed into a woman, then back into a man; he suggests a psychic wholeness in aging. Twentieth-century literature offers such active and creative portraits as Gully Jimson of Joyce Cary's trilogy (*Herself Surprised, To Be a Pilgrim,* and *The Horse's Mouth*).

The few older women portrayed in classical literature and myth are usually manifestations of evil—the fearsome old witch, for example. Those positive examples that come to mind, such as St. Anne, are often peripheral to the institutions from which they come; in fact, like many Protestants, I never heard of St. Anne until I went to graduate school, where I studied Leonardo da Vinci's paintings of her with Mary and Christ. Nevertheless, an archetype of the Wise Old Woman does exist. Curious about the dimensions of this figure, I have combed various disciplines, particularly gerontology, to uncover the image of the aged matriarch that has remained unarticulated in the female collective unconscious. I believe that although women have lived out the Wise Old Woman archetype, they have not spoken or written about it enough to make the general culture aware of its existence.

One image that is helpful in constructing a positive archetype of the older woman is the Greek goddess Demeter. A goddess of the ancient Greeks, Demeter was, among other things, the goddess of the seasons. She had one daughter, Persephone; various possible fathers are cited in different myths, but Demeter is never portrayed as married, nor is Persephone's father ever depicted with her. Demeter and Persephone became central figures to the mother/daughter rites of the Eleusinian mysteries.

According to the myths, Hades snatched Persephone and took her underground to be his bride. Up until this time there was no winter. The earth gave forth her fruits in a constant state of spring and summer. When Demeter lost Persephone to Hades, she grieved for her, and this brought on winter. Thus, the ancients explained the seasons by saying that when Persephone is underground with Hades, Demeter grieves and winter reigns, but when she is released to her mother, spring comes and then summer, until she must go underground to her husband Hades again when fall comes.

The myth demands a broader concept of mothering than just a relationship between the mother and the young girl through adolescence. Demeter cares for Persephone as a young girl, but the maiden is also returned to her mother for part of the year all her life, suggesting how the mother/daughter dyad continues to bear psychic fruit for all of Demeter's life. Also, when Persephone disappears into marriage with Hades, Demeter's caretaking beyond kinship roles enters into this archetype.

Although Demeter continually searches for her daughter/self, she stops to nurse the infant Demophoön, whom she makes almost totally invulnerable by dipping him into fire. This suggests the disinterested caretaker who nurses and goes her way, unlike the mother caretaker whose life is forever entwined with her young and who would probably find it too painful to harden her young in the way that teachers and nurses might find necessary.

The aged Demeter blends with the gnostic concept of the Sophia, the sister-wife-anima who helped God create the world, to form an image of a loving and protective matriarch. Toward the end of his life, Jung postulated that all archetypes blend into one another like the colors in the spectrum; the different feminine archetypes or life routes that various women have lived through do often seem to merge almost imperceptibly into one another in later life, coalescing in the image of the aged Demeter/Sophia.

The archetype of the Wise Old Woman rests on various roles of younger women that enact aspects of the Demeter myth, from mothering to nursing biologically unrelated but needy others. The Demeter archetype thus contains a wide spectrum of caretaking, which gives the woman psychic riches. Women are very nurturing, even toward their friends. These skills and lessons in nurturing are the bedrock of matriarchal wisdom, what Carol Gilligan, a pioneering and insightful writer on women's morality and life stages, calls the woman's "morality of responsibility"—as opposed to men's "morality of rights," which emphasizes "separation rather than attachment . . . [and] the individual rather than the relationship as primary."[1]

Using the Demeter/Sophia archetype as a way to examine older women is anathema to many social scientists who usually shy away from imagistic and subjective ways of knowing such as mythology, archetypal psychology, or dream material. Gerontology is dominated by the fields of medical services and sociology, disciplines that objectify and quantify the groups they study. They study action, or behavior, as if it were in fact psyche. Practitioners in both fields also generally take it for granted that all human traits are enculturated rather than innate. These researchers too often excise from the human being a sense of soul, individual uniqueness, and free will. All *yang* and no *yin*, they unknowingly worship Apollo, the god of the sun, whose unrelenting light scorches and burns up the dark, the moist, and the inner recesses of being. Apollo is also the god of youth and god of the bow, which stands for his analytic faculty that cuts and kills from a distance. He is juxtaposed by some classicists to Dionysus, who loved the dark, the irrational, the orgiastic, and lived surrounded by his female followers.

In *The Myth of Analysis*, James Hillman shows how modern Western scientific consciousness is an unconscious acting-out of the masculine Apollonian consciousness, for "it belongs to youth, it kills from a distance (its distance kills), and, keeping the scientific cut of objectivity, it never merges with or marries its material."[2] It is a structure of consciousness that has "an estranged relation with the feminine." Similarly, certain of the most prestigious gerontologists can often see women only as masculine counterparts, as objects, or as the Other. They do not realize how "other" women really are and insist on seeing them as mirror reflections of themselves.

An important gerontologist who has done cross-cultural studies, David Gutmann, exemplifies this way of seeing women. He describes powerful older women as matriarchs, a term that to him implies that older women are imperialistic or hierarchical in their approach to other people, in the way that patriarchs have traditionally been.[3] Gutmann's fear of women also shows in a published section of his dialogue with gerontologists and feminists at Ann Arbor, Michigan, in which he says that the movement of women in search of work and self outside the home has been responsible for increasing child abuse.[4] Not only is there no evidence for this; his statement is a typically Apollonian form of projecting the violent and dismembering aspects of human behavior onto women.

Women researchers cannot always be counted on for fairer presentations. Bernice L. Neugarten derives most of her ideas about our cultural conceptions of the aged from the stories people make up about certain pictures. Yet the pictures she uses are intrinsically sexist and naturally provoke polarized descriptions of men and women.[5] The dominating figure in one picture is an older man with a pipe in his hand—the symbol of a gentle, kindly, contemplative male. He is standing in back of and over an older woman, whose face we cannot even see—she is *literally effaced*. A young woman stands next to the older man, but in front of her is a seated young man, in profile, gesturing and apparently talking. Thus, the masculine principle dominates the picture; the feminine is quiet and hidden. The young man is active and vital; the young woman is quiescent, standing in back of him in a passive, receptive mode quite different from that of the older man in back of the older woman. Neugarten remarks that the picture is almost always perceived as a family, which I think simply reflects an ordinary contextual perception. What would happen with a picture with four men, or a picture of four women?

Even critics within the social sciences are questioning "an ideology that attempts to mystify the social relations of the knower and the known through procedures that appear anonymous and impersonal."[6] It seems that the respondents in such "objective" studies as Neugarten's are responding to the unconscious projections of the researchers, yet all the data are treated as the respondents' *own* projections of the images of men and women.

Nevertheless, so long as one realizes that unconscious fantasies often lie beneath the researchers' hypotheses, data-gathering, and interpretations, gerontological studies yield significant and provocative ideas and images. For example, most of the studies of differences between older men and women suggest divergent paths of development for each sex. Since even cross-cultural studies reflect this finding, a strong argument can be made for instinctive unfolding in the older person of traits traditionally assigned to the opposite sex. This urge, which appears to surface in both older men and women, could be called the archetype of wholeness. That is, the psyche corrects its one-sidedness as it moves through the later stages of life. This seems to be an innate and autonomous internal process, which is exciting and reassuring; the personality unfolds and completes itself regardless of cultural or familial repression. Through studying the elderly personality, we may come to see that the given strengths of the individual psyche are at least as important as external formative influences.

The qualities of older men seem to provide the norm for the "disengagement" model of old age that has so dominated gerontology, probably because this theory is simple, neat, and satisfies the unconscious wish widespread in our society that old people would not only die unseen but would even reassure us they are happy in their demise. Older white males, the major group studied in the formation of this theory, appear to be more "femininely" passive than younger men, although recent research shows that they are perhaps more internally active, more reflective, and more interested in communal feelings than ever before. Yet disengagement theory has it that well-adjusted old people just fade out into death, automatically relinquishing their roles and involvement. It is typical of our extroverted and materialistic culture to call an introspective, meditative time of life by a derogatory term such as *disengagement*. This theory reflects also how little young researchers understand older people. Again, remember the Apollonian archetype. The younger researcher's relative lack of complexity and maturity gives him or her a detachment, an estranging judgment, that denies the older male's deeper and more meditative view of the world.

Another popular theory that reflects the same prejudice is the "activity" theory; here researchers measure the activities of older people and assume that the more active they are, the happier they are. Older men appear to "fail" according to this theory, but only in a society that measures engagement by social or physical activity. Actually, some research indicates that such men are engaging with other human beings and themselves at a deeper level than they probably ever did before. This is an intrapsychic or subjective, inner mode of delving, a voyage into the labyrinth of self and relationships. David Gutmann says that "older men are more interested in love than in conquest or power, more interested in community than in agency . . . they are more diffusely sensual, more sensitive to the incidental pleasures and pains of the world."[7] Another researcher says that older males score higher than younger males on "warmth/expressiveness."[8] Still another says that older men are "more tolerant of their nurturant and affiliative" qualities, and that through the age of fifty-four men dominate within marriage, but after fifty-five women do.[9] Notice the underlying hierarchical fantasy; one could just as well say that the husband begins to take comfort in being the one contained and cared for in the relationship, or that the wife begins to relate more actively with the outside world.

In any case, older men are clearly still vital and active, but in an internal sense. They are assimilating the qualities they denied as young men; they are growing, correcting one-sidedness. As they become more like women, older men become more humane, more complex—more human, in the finest sense of the word.

The qualities of older women are more difficult to trace, because, for one thing, few researchers use women as their sample. The white male is still the model for research, even in gerontology, which is curious considering how much longer women live. Even when women are included in the sample, sometimes so-called anomalous women—professional women, or older single women—are left out. This is the "Hera syndrome" that many male researchers fall prey to; they can only conceive of the older woman as a wife, contained within the family.

However, Dr. Marilyn Bell has amassed a body of yet unpublished research, some of which shows that older women have many innate assets for a healthy, psychologically satisfying old age. My survey of the research certainly suggests that women have numerous types of *intra*psychic strengths that develop as they grow older. First of all, women become more extroverted. Japanese[10] and Italian[11] studies agree on this conclusion of many American researchers; even Gutmann says that "women become more aggressive in later life, less sentimental, and more managerial."[12] Gutmann is sometimes fearful of this tendency, as are some other male researchers. Thompson, for example, lapses into an apprehensive fantasy about Amazons, making odd statements such as "Many of the female species are gradually becoming hunters in their own right and will voyage wherever they will." He sees nothing natural, in terms of biological evolution, about women's endurance and emotional strength and guesses that these qualities came about because of "an excessive radiation period," an accident of fate. Nevertheless, he, too, says that women remain "more intact, more intelligent, more capable of sustaining object relations, and often have a maternal lifetime background of caring for those who are in need of help."[13] Thus, even male researchers who seem uncomfortable with their findings emphasize older women's strength, energy, and independence.

One important thing that male researchers do not often realize is that the more managerial, controlling older woman makes her decisions about others on a foundation of caring she developed as a younger woman. She sees individuals more clearly, more contextually, than men generally do. Thus, the older woman bases her greater decisiveness on a compassion and a sense of others that make her leadership qualitatively different from men's. It is not that women move *beyond* relatedness into personal autonomy as they grow older; rather, the earlier and more traditional feminine role transforms and extends older women into a more dynamic and catalytic role within society. Their relatedness becomes less tied to personal circles and encompasses larger groups.

Women, of course, learn their basic approach to life long before they become mothers (if they do). Every woman has lived out the Persephone archetype in her earliest years of development. Women learn the value and techniques of relationships from their mothers in a more direct, imagistic, and intimate way than their brothers do.[14]

Even women's acclaimed "fear of success" syndrome has recently been reexamined and found to reflect a cooperative, symbiotic view of achievement; women are not afraid to achieve when the achievement does not mean that others will suffer.[15] This less hierarchical, more *eros*-dominated basis to women's morality is probably the bedrock of the Wise Old Woman archtype. Feminine relatedness is primary in matriarchal values and is, I believe, a basis for a fulfilling old age for a woman.

An unhappy paradox for men in old age is that when they most value and want loving relationships, they are usually unskilled at keeping alive their relationships even with their children. Women, on the other hand, are far more able to maintain significance and importance in their children's and family's lives. There is some evidence, in fact, that relationships among lower-class women are almost totally located in the family, especially among the female members.[16] Eva Kahana, a gerontologist who studies family structure, says that grandparenthood is carried along maternal lines of descent and that grandmothers are more actively involved with their grandchildren than are grandfathers. She also analyzes the importance and closeness of older women's relationships with their daughters and sisters.[17]

Women also tend to create lifelong bonds with other women outside of their families. Middle- and upper-class women find much continuity in their lives through their friendships with other women.[18] One researcher, Beth Hess, says that during marriage, women select friends twice as often as men do, and that wives select their friends as often from their own locale as from among wives of their husbands' business friends.[19] This latter point seems important to me, as it suggests that there is a commonality of interests among women — that women can connect with one another simply by virtue of being in the same place. Those researchers who have studied older lesbians appear to confirm this. Deborah Wolf describes the San Francisco lesbian community as "influenced by feminist ideology . . . and more socialist in nature." She shows that the lesbian women experience themselves as a community because they live in the same area.[20] She sees the male counterpart as capitalist, competitive, and flamboyant. What she calls socialist could also be described as a deep, loving connection with one another. She says, for example, that very often old lovers become close friends after "cooling off."[21]

Ann Holder and Marvin Ernst also see lesbians as more pyschologically, emotionally, and spiritually involved with one another than male homosexuals are. They say that homosexual men usually see love as episodic, but women see love as a major driving force.[22]

Many of these studies suggest that a full acceptance of feminine roles is at least as important as the mode of development urged through the popular idea of androgyny. James Hillman says that all successful psychoanalysis concludes — which is the point at which creative and fruitful individuation can begin — when the feminine principle is elevated out of its position of inferiority both within the psyche and in the outer world.[23] This is true for women and for men; women must embrace all that the feminine principle embodies. Studies that investigate older women's earlier lives suggest that the more younger women live out their gender roles, the more able they are as older women to assimilate and live out opposite sexual roles. In her study of an apartment house tenanted by old women, Arlie Russell Hochschild found that most of the women usually kept peer and kin ties separate, but that those closest to their families were the most active in peer society; for most of these women, daughters and granddaughters were the kin with whom they identified most closely. Furthermore, their visitors were usually daughters and daughters-in-law (which certainly belies the unloved mother-in-law stereotype).[24]

Thus, women seem to be singularly blessed in terms of their relationships with each other. These relationships constitute what I call "underground matrilinearism." Women's culture is seen by many scholars as transmitted through oral traditions; men move theirs forward by means of the written word, making it more apparent and "real" than female culture. While cultural continuity seems based on patriarchal structures, women find their matrix of continuity through less official, nonverbalized bonding with one another, which is "underground" in the sense that most men and many women do not consciously recognize the force and coherence of these intergenerational and peer bonds. This is one face of the Wise Old Woman. She reaps the harvests of Demeter, of her having cared for others throughout most of her life. She has learned to love and connect deeply with other human beings. There are many possible causes behind this pattern. Women who do not have children often end up in what we call the helping professions, so that even her work can give a woman Demeter-like maternal concerns about others. Remember that as a nurse and nursemaid, Demeter extended her caretaking skills to the community at large.

Because the older woman has been so deeply engaged in earlier stages of her life in caring for frail or new life, she has lasting roots in her relationships with those for whom she cared. This is especially apparent in portraits of grandmothers and mothers in women's autobiographies.[25] The older woman often can intuit others' problems and personalities more quickly and accurately than others can, and move into new relationships when she needs to. She is more experienced and probably innately better at forging bonds between people than older men are.

Thus, when one examines women's image of the matriarch, a different pattern emerges from the one that Gutmann portrays. By the term *matriarchy*, women usually mean feminine culture and the generations of women through which each woman traces her identity as reflected by the Eleusinian rites. This culture is exclusively female, but it is not antagonistic to men, as men such as Daniel Patrick Moynihan (in his work on black women) have named it. The matriarch embodies the opposite of the dominating, conquering elements of the patriarch. She is responsible and protective, as presented in Käthe Kollwitz's art or Toni Morrison's novels. The old and weathered matriarch guards and contains those more vulnerable than herself. She has arrived at a "universal moral perspective," the "morality of responsibility" which eschews "the infliction of hurt." This latter immorality becomes central to her concern. Because of her close study of relationships throughout her life, she has "an insistent contextual relativism," and a strong and vital sense "of being responsible to the world."[26] In an interview, Toni Morrison agreed with this in her definition of the black matriarch as "a parent, as a sort of umbrella figure, culture-bearer . . . with not just her children but with all children"; Morrison emphasizes this woman's "huge responsibilities" and her crucial presence in terms of the survival of many of the children.[27]

Yet a woman is also more independent and autonomous in later life than she is earlier in her life cycle. I like to trace the roots of psychic being in the Greek deities Hestia and Hermes, often paired in ancient thought. Hestia is the goddess of the hearth, contained by the household and containing the family; this archetype is the one with which older men seem to want to connect. Older women, on the other hand, seem to wish to connect with the Hermes aspect of their psychic roots; Hermes is the messenger god—always on the road, symbol of the mercurial, exploring, fluid part of deity. Gerontologists sometimes remark on the "eccentric" or "bizarre" behavior of older women, and perhaps fittingly so: Hermes is also the archetype of the trickster, unashamed of and connecting with all sides of the self. Like Hestia, he is one of the "inferior" gods among the Olympians. He does not dwell in the great palace on the mountain, but is forever roving the country, bringing messages to the gods. Older women, too, are movers, whereas younger women are often somewhat cloistered by their roles as mother (Demeter), wife (Hera), and homemaker (Hestia). Freed of these responsibilities, women can take on more active roles, embodied in such figures as Artemis, the huntress who comes to the aid of women in childbirth and who prevails in a realm that exists apart from relationships with men.[28] Artemis' virginity can be seen as a psychic purity, an autonomy that dedicates itself entirely to the task at hand. Hestia, too, was thought to be a virgin goddess; she embodies a selfless devotion to the home, while Artemis has a purity of devotion toward her own pursuits and toward needy persons outside the family circle.

Athena represents another feminine archetype that is especially noticeable in older women. Athena is a sister to rulers and wayfaring men, an extroverted helper who infuses feminine values into the patriarchal realm. She, too, is a virgin. She carries a shield, which emphasizes her ego strength and invulnerability. The civic wisdom of Athena surfaces especially in such older women as Golda Meir and Margaret Thatcher, both great political leaders. Whereas in *The Great Mother* Erich Neumann celebrates the Sophia archetype as representing the contemplative and passive yet earthly wisdom of the mature woman, the active, Athena archetype is at least as common. As Mary Daly suggests in *Gyn-Ecology*, we should restore to the term *crone* its connotations of holy fury and knowledge. We could also call the active, fiercely independent side of older women the Aged Amazon or Active Wisdom.

Two studies especially reflect the independence of the Wise Old Woman. In her research on frail elderly women, Vira Kivett shows that "self-rated health and adequacy of transportation are more important to quality of life than other selected factors and account for a greater amount of difference in subjective well-being."[29] Out of eighty-two women aged seventy-five to ninety-nine who lived in their own homes, the majority wanted to live *alone* though near relatives; their self-rated health was more important than their actual health. This seems important, because high morale can often overcome, or even cure, poor health. Except for health, these women's autonomy, as symbolized by access to transportation, was the *most important thing* to them. Though most were very poor, only 11 percent could think of services they needed. Kivett remarks on how these women "reflect tenacity" in maintaining home ownership and living alone.

Helena Lopata also found a desire to live alone in widows.[30] Margaret Feldman, on the other hand, studied a group of mothers and daughters living together and found some rather psychically harrowing situations. The mothers were twice as likely as mothers not living with their daughters to see themselves as their daughters' children, and the daughters were much less globally happy than the mothers.[31] "Global" happiness sounds euphoric and childlike; one wonders if a mother who has given over responsibility for her self to her daughter has not also given up some important last steps in individuation.

We can return to the Demeter myth to diagnose the problem here. Demeter and her adult daughter, Persephone, have homes apart from one another; their time together consists of visiting and of redefining their relationship as they develop in different ways. But they always part again. Thus, the older mother living with her daughter is perhaps not only making her child unhappy but also reversing the process of her own independence, settling instead for a rather dubious return to childlike dependence.

It is important to note here that research shows that warmth and expressiveness are moral and desirable for both older men and women, but that almost all older women prefer personal autonomy to earlier helping roles. Older women find such roles quite stifling. They want to explore the larger world. Researchers believe that this preference is quite conscious.[32] It is not that older women reject loving and caring, but that unknown worlds both within and without press into their awareness. Many older women also undoubtedly feel the competence that their life experience brings, and they naturally want to bring their special talents to fruition in the world.

Finally, I see a new future as each sex embraces positive traits usually ascribed to the other and as the older woman enters our culture more fully. As the older woman becomes more visible, the feminine principle will enter more strongly into culture as a whole. This will be helpful to younger women, who will see examples of future selves that are free of child-care and domestic responsibilities but still reflect and garner the rewards from their former selves. As older women begin more openly to express their aberrant, eccentric selfhood, feminine individuality will become valued by and part of the culture. Women's ability to love and relate deeply, to value other people and to protect them, will perhaps become part of public policy as stronger and more forceful older women gain and retain their place in the public sphere.

If women knew that their energy would surge in their middle years and that this energy would help them expand their influence into the larger community, they could ready themselves and look forward to the epic tasks they will tackle in the future, whereas now they more often waste their energy on menopausal problems. Much of women's supposed mid-life crisis may be caused by cultural biases that convolute the energy that presses older women into the world. The witch archetype may be a male response to the threat of women who have lived long enough to manifest a fierce selfhood. Instead of tranquilizers, women need tasks through which the energy can stream into the world with their accumulated wisdom.

The urge to action is there, often to the surprise of the woman herself. In *The Measure of My Days*, Florida Scott-Maxwell says:

"Age puzzles me. I thought it was a quiet time. My seventies were interesting, and fairly serene, but my eighties are passionate. I grow more intense as I age. To my own surprise I burst out with hot conviction. Only a few years ago I enjoyed my tranquility, now I am disturbed by the outer world and by human quality in general, so that I want to put things right as though I still owed a debt to life. I must calm down. I am far too frail to indulge in moral fervour . . . all this is very tiring, but love at any age takes everything you've got."[33]

Her tiredness did not stop this older woman from writing a powerful book of meditations on life. Colette's last book, *The Blue Lantern*, written when she was in her late seventies, is very similar in form and theme. The metaphysical depth of these books and the extent of the authors' social engagement make the protagonists of these works important role models for older women, embodying the gerontological finding that "as women reach the last phase of life, they leave behind many of the crises of the middle years, turning their attention to a new range of developmental tasks."[34]

5. Old Age and Death: More Aspects of Feminine Transformation

The experience of death is a difficult thing to write of, for we can go only as far as the imagination can take us. A very limited number of cases in which people have "died," left the body, and then returned have been documented,[1] but it is difficult to ascertain the extent to which these experiences are hallucinatory or real. We also have the reports of those who regularly attend to those who are dying, but we can only guess at how much of what they go through the dying are actually able to explain.[2]

Our actual experience of any event is largely determined by the imagery with which we anticipate it. Our images of death and godhead are then a major influence on our attitude toward the last stage of life. For the most part, the masculine view of godhead and of death prevails in our culture. In a recent anthology called *Death and Society,* a chaplain, Robert E. Neale, discusses his image of the godhead behind death:

The god of the Hospice is a god with everlasting arms and overflowing breasts. It is a god of powerful comfort. The image contrasts with one presented in a ballet of the prodigal son. At the end of the story, the son finds his way home. The father stands at one corner of the stage. He is large, stern, immobile. The son crawls across the stage to his father. The passage seems interminable. He reaches his father's feet. He looks up. The father remains large, stern, immobile. The son takes another eternity to pull himself up into his father's folded arms. When he finally reaches the arms, his father cradles him and effortlessly carries him home. This god is a father and lord, concerned about obedience, sin, confession, judgment. Yet, this god also touches, feeds, and loves his children. The God of the Judaic-Christian tradition is both these gods. Because of my experience at the Hospice, my God now has breasts. But the hair on His chest remains. And the everlasting arms are sometimes vehicles for fists. Even so, this God weeps.[3]

Here is a man who senses the feminine element of death as a containing, loving force; yet with masculine arrogance, he assimilates the feminine, grafting and so subsuming the comforting breasts and arms of the mother to the body of the cruel and punishing father. This author also mistrusts the peaceful last stages of dying, suggesting later in the essay that Freudian research should be done on "regression, dependency, orality, identification, transference and counter-transference, and idealization" in dying. He feels that the serenity of the dying is "regression" and that the dying should be helped to a more active stage in the "service of the ego."[4]

Contrasting with Neale's image of death is Judith Bardwick's in her book *In Transition:*

It seems to me that men and women connect with the great events of death and of birth differently. I believe that women are closer to the creation of life and to blood and thereby to dying, and that women are more prone to protect, nurture, and create bonds than are men. Women's love is more likely to involve protection, tenderness, and commitment. My image is not passive or pastoral but grand. In the garden of the Museum of Modern Art in New York there is a statue of a great, nude, heroic woman. This figure is Power, the Mother of Us All, the Knower of Mysteries, Mother Earth. It suggests the ultimate base and the firmament; it belongs within the cycle of creation and destruction, of life and death . . . the last and best mystery is, if women create life, then do women control death? . . . I have given life and in this way I am familiar with death. This knowledge is the wellspring of my connectedness. This knowledge I share with men, this *experience* I share with women.[5]

The artist Käthe Kollwitz also presents a unique vision of death. In her last series of lithographs she depicts death as a friend to the aging and ailing. The best on this subject is her 1921 woodcut *Death with Woman in Lap,* which features death as a "great maternal protector." Death is seen as a female twice in Kollwitz's later lithographs, and all the victims of death in her last series are adult women who respond with "equanimity or reverence."[6] Kollwitz's portraits of herself in old age gently but absolutely refute Freudian notions of serenity as regression:

> In her self-portraits she confronts the aging woman. She speaks to the sense of truth, for every line and wrinkle, every over-burdened shoulder is, also, woman — in her pain and, finally, in her glorious dignity: not as young, lively, beautiful in the prettiness of health, but as the eternal "I will" of the spirit.[7]

Bardwick and Kollwitz represent two very different kinds of minds — the scientist and the artist. Yet their images of godhead and final truths are based on the same kinds of feminine experience.

GENDER DIFFERENCES IN IMAGES OF DEATH

In 1971 Kurt W. Back began research on how different age groups perceive time and death.[8] Back sampled 502 Americans aged forty-five to seventy. He found only a few differences among age groups, the most important being that younger people saw time as having a "static quality" and "somewhat subdued emotional tone," preferring images such as a quiet ocean, while older people saw "time as a more rushing kind of event." Back was surprised to find that gender was much more important than age in determining perceptions of time and death. Women saw time "like a whirlwind, a bird in flight, a rapidly weaving cloth." Older women were more aware than older men of the quality and rapid passage of time in the later years of life.

Back concluded that women's images of time are merely more active than men's, a rather limited interpretation. More significant surely is the cyclic nature of the women's time images. This is typical of the spiritual dynamics of matriarchy and is antithetical to masculine perceptions of time and to traditional Christianity, which treats seasonal time as a result of the Fall. Back thought that men see time as a diffused event: they conceptualize it as a "large revolving wheel, a road leading over the hill, an old man with a cane, wind-driven sand, and an old woman spinning." Almost all of those images reflect a feeling that time is linear; all the images are "going some place" except for the last one. It is not certain whether the large revolving wheel is like the wheel of fortune, standing for the great round of birth, life, and death (which would make it cyclical), or whether it is moving forward in space (which would make it linear). The old man with a cane can be interpreted as the debilitated male self (ego and libido). The wind-driven sand represents chaotic helplessness. Both images reflect the masculine sense of time as destructive, alienating, and also perhaps emasculating. The women's images of time seem more clearly similar, less ambiguous: "a whirlwind, a bird in flight, a rapidly weaving cloth." On one item each the men's and women's categories cross over; the women's bird in flight may be seen as an image of linear time just as the men's revolving wheel may be cyclical. Yet the major imagery of each sex is sharply different.

It is significant that women see time as the actual product of the process of weaving, while men imagine time as the weaver herself. Traditionally, women have been the weavers. Circe and Calypso, two of the women who attempt to delay Odysseus from returning to his wife Penelope (weaver of shrouds), present themselves to him as weavers. While there are a few instances of men imagining weaving women as good forces, they have generally imagined the woman weaver as evil. The image of woman as a nefarious weaver, a sort of human Arachne, is widespread in Renaissance literature. And, of course, the archetypal weaver is Athena, who changed her human weaving competitor, Arachne, into a spider. Men apparently fear these archetypes; they see the woman who weaves the strands of life into a meaningful fabric as an enchantress who can create life, decide its duration, and end it as in the myth of the three sisters who spin, measure, and cut the yarn of life.

On the other hand, women see pattern and meaning as the products that life and time weave; they do not project onto any particular person or group any fault or responsibility for the products. Furthermore, if one sees time as cyclical, as a process — a bird in the midst of flight, a whirlwind, cloth that is forming a pattern as fast as the thread creates it — then one's own life cycle is less fearful, since it can be seen within the context of a process that is meaningful.

Back's study also revealed that women see death as a "gently-veiled lady, an understanding doctor, a falling curtain, and the end of a song." The latter image makes one's life a work of spiritual artistry; all the images are poignant and sympathetic. The images of the curtain and the veil also suggest that death is not necessarily an end to individual existence. These images impart a quiet and gentle mystery to the concept of death. Men, on the other hand, imagine death as a "grinning butcher, a hangman with bloody hands, and a crumbling tower." The last image is perhaps the saddest, suggesting that men identify their being with a kind of doomed and static phallus. Nature, who crumbles the tower, wastes it away, is an antagonist. Like the weaving woman, nature may be a feminine death agent, and the image of the tower suggests how alien nature is to men—the tower is inorganic, nontransformative. Also sadly, men project violence and the power to mutilate onto male figures. Back comments that death is a personal opponent for them, while women sometimes even reflect what he calls the "Harlequin factor," a cluster of images of death as a lover.

While Back's study is fascinating, it is limited in three ways. First, such testing would have been of more general value if it had been cross-cultural. Canadians insist that American culture is implicitly more Freudian than theirs, which they say is more mythic and Jungian; perhaps Back's work reflects the deep Oedipal anguish and separation of American men. Second, Back created the images and his subjects chose among them, so that the women in his sample had to choose from images that were male-generated. His choice of "understanding doctor," for example, imposes his value system of a benevolent patriarchy. I suspect women might imagine death as a nurse, not as a male authority figure who overpowers the passive female. Third, Back does not understand the significance of the images themselves, which have essences that reverberate differently in the psyches of women and men.

Back's insights into male concepts of death are borne out by current male writing on the subject, however. Paul Ramsey, professor of religion at Princeton University, has written a central and definitive article on the meaning of death and the appropriate stance toward it. He equates humanism with the dread of death, which he sees as an incomparable indignity. Acceptance of death, he feels, comes from two antihumanist attitudes: the rejection of bodily life, which generates indifference to a person before his or her death, and the rejection of the unique importance of each individual. He calls death the enemy, saying that "death is *never* a part of life" and insisting that fear of death is appropriate because it is the dread of oblivion, of there being only empty room in one's stead."[9]

A recent book by James Hillman, *The Dream and the Under-world,* reflects again the masculine existential nausea that so often turns away from the final stage of life and rejects death as lacking any essential meaning. Ramsey's oblivion and empty-room metaphor are strongly echoed in this final passage from Hillman's book:

> Dreams are sleep's watchful brother, of death's fraternity, heralds, watchmen of that coming night, and our attitude toward them may be modeled upon Hades, receiving, hospitable, yet relentlessly deepening, attuned to the nocturne, dusky, and with a fearful cold intelligence that gives permanent shelter in his house to the incurable conditions of human being.[10]

The mythic god Hades, or Pluto, may be a specifically masculine version of death. He mutilates the earth, rends a chasm out of which he rises to snatch Persephone, the daughter of ongoingness, and takes her underground; in Hillman's passage, Hades is pulling us all underground to a dark, cold, permanent burial place. The only answer to our neurotic condition is death, who is a male, and his brother sleep who nightly assaults the human psyche with ultimately indecipherable warnings of annihilation. Hillman seems to suffer from a failure of nerve, while Judith Bardwick, a psychologist of about the same age, presents an image of death as a goddess — a large, powerful, cosmic affirmation.

THE CULTURAL AND ACTUAL DIFFERENCES BETWEEN MEN'S AND WOMEN'S DEATHS

All men are not unable to imagine death as women do. However, the majority of male authors do seem to view death as the great antagonist, often depicting older men as heroic because they fight their own deaths: King Lear and Saul Bellow's Herzog are good examples. In fact, the Lolita complex is another manifestation of this; old men see their age as an attack on their selfhood and sexuality and seek ever younger women to reflect potency and youth.

Of course, culturally acknowledged heroic deaths have been forced upon men, certainly a negative indoctrination. Young men have fearful and gruesome military deaths held up to them as achievements of masculinity; murder is even a part of self-definition, as when a man murders the lover of his wife or the wife herself. The killing of large animals such as cattle has usually been a masculine duty, as has hunting. Boys have been systematically taught to use weapons in almost all cultures. The heroic death of the young warrior is considered desirable in some circles.

The death of a young woman, on the other hand, is a universal cultural taboo, like the death of children. The natural deaths of old women have not hitherto been written of, because women's deaths are a foreign domain to men. Women's images and fantasies of their own deaths are a new force being brought to the surface of human consciousness. How much the images are nature and how much nurture is unclear, but probably the images relate to innate and essential differences between women and men. Women have usually died out of the public eye, which may make boys and girls imagine their deaths quite differently. When I imagine my foremothers' deaths (other than because of old age), I see witches burned at the stake or mothers dying giving birth.

Even a woman who dies at the hands of a killer-rapist usually dies alone. The image of the witch, though depicting a public death, is difficult for most women to identify with; it bears the stigma of the criminal. The other images suggest that women's deaths evolve specifically and concretely from their sex. Their imagery of death is the opposite of male imagery of public, heroic deaths. Women generally imagine their deaths as a private, isolated, and intimate event; the return of the body to its elements of earth and water is also comforting for women, since it means a return of the self to those elements that symbolize feminine identity and individuation. The images of death that one carries, then, are undoubtedly enculturated as well as innate.

WOMEN AS BIRTH/DEATH ATTENDANTS

Women often accompany the ill to the thresholds of their deaths. Michelangelo's *Pieta* is an image that embodies this consoling, sad, yet nurturing figure. It is an image that has been claimed, however, for dying sons, not daughters. A more powerful image for women occurs in Ingmar Bergman's *Cries and Whispers,* where a young woman dying of cancer is cradled against the nude large-breasted maid who has nursed her for several months. The position is reminiscent both of Michelangelo's *Pieta* and of a nursing mother.

This image, as much as any other, depicts the great seriousness with which women take up relationships; women are more "grave" because they have always been privy to the secrets of birth, death, and rebirth.

It is not an accident that women dominate the research and services in gerontology. Some sociologists guess that this is because as an oppressed group, women identify with the socially ostracized elderly.[11] They attribute this to female reaction formation based on the cultural inferiority of women.

Robert A. Neale, the hospice chaplain quoted earlier, projects devouring instincts onto the women who work within the hospice:

> It took me several months to realize fully that I was surrounded by women for the first time in my life. Not only are the nurses female, but so also are the doctors and the director of the Hospice. There were and are two male psychiatrists and a male chaplain, but members of these professions are hardly noted for possession of masculine traits and concerns. It is not enough to note also that these women are dedicated and competent. It is to be noted also that they are, by and large, middle-aged, buxom, and single.[12]

He portrays these women as devouring mother figures who cause the dying to regress. The fact that they are middle-aged, buxom, and single signifies their sexual repression; Neale suggests that their sublimated sexual energy represses the ego strength of the dying. He even rejects the few males in the hospice as not possessed of so-called "masculine traits and concerns" which would, he thinks, clearly awaken the dying out of their lethargy. Neale seems to think the women are getting sexual gratification through providing a maternal image. In his book *The Great Mother,* Erich Neumann discusses this male projection of the devouring and deadly mother.[13] This image of woman is probably specific to the masculine unconscious. Not all men share it, but many people see one side of mothering as deadly and devouring.

There are positive explanations, however, for the frequent association with and presence of women at death. Women have and will undoubtedly continue to minister over birth and death, the entry and the exit. In his book *Touching,* which discusses how maternal gratification of the infant's tactile needs influences individuation and humanity, Ashley Montagu discusses cultures in which the dying are held as children in a mother's arms.[14] Women have always nursed the dying, and they are returning as midwives to their rightful place beside the birthing mother. Even now, with the Western male monopoly on obstetrics, the majority of all children in the world are delivered by women. In the past, doctors, practically all male, have been notorious for their failure to tend the dying; it is women, and too often strangers in a hospital, who attend the dying. With many more women now becoming physicians, maybe things will change. Perhaps these women will retain their ability to nurture the dying and teach their male compatriots more compassion. It is significant that the pioneer of contemporary studies of death, Elizabeth Kübler-Ross, developed many of her ideas while nursing the newly freed inmates of the concentration camps of World War II. She recognized the hopeful and affirmative imagery that even these souls portrayed in their last messages to the world, such as the butterflies drawn on the walls of the barracks. Kübler-Ross's feminine sensibility and intuitive intelligence undoubtedly found a good channel in her nursing activities, and she recognized traits in the dying that most men probably would not have.

Studies are just now beginning to document the more highly developed patience and ability to perceive fine modulations in mood and voice that females demonstrate even in infancy.[15] Jung has been labeled sexist for his recognition of the superior ability of women in relating, yet this ability clearly exists and underlies much of women's quest through life. Women are superior caretakers. Taking care of other people as they die may be the most spiritual act a human being ever does.

Women may also be particularly interested in old age because that is the stage of life that affords them a greater freedom and a special kind of individuation. Women may intuit the importance of the last stage of life and the need to protect its parameters more than men do. Women are less prone than men are to identify their work outside the home as the most or the only productive aspect of their lives. *All* the years of the lifespan yield growth and ripening.

Women's experience of their bodies also affects their attitude toward death. Much recent feminist literature embraces the *tabula rasa* model for the human psyche, insisting that all aspects of mothering are learned and that men can easily be trained to be primary caretakers.[16] Yet current work on the meaning of birth in terms of mother-infant bonding and lactation, and even some rather esoteric work on introjection of the mother's attitudes to the fetus, suggests that women's biological ability to give birth has enormous psychic and spiritual ramifications. But whether a woman chooses to give birth or not, she still inhabits a body that gives her an experience of nature and incarnation that is markedly different from a man's. Inhabiting a body that can give birth influences women's sense of the meaning of death. For instance, one of my friends had a recurring dream while she was caring for her dying mother; she dreamed she was giving birth by pulling a baby girl out of a pool of water. Death and birth seem thus to be more integral in the feminine psyche.

The psychological symbiosis that exists between mother and daughter also partially underlies the feminine attitude toward death. Recall that female patients who remembered their own birth through LSD therapy could not tell if they were experiencing their own or their children's birth. If in giving birth a daughter experiences her own birth from her mother's point of view, then she may also gain foreknowledge of her own death as she nurses her mother toward death. Grof's work also proves that psychic rebirth or transformation must be preceded by the death of the ego; perhaps the death of one's mother, the embodiment of the matriarchal superego and ego, is for women symbolic foreknowledge of the ego's death. Gerontologists speak of the sexism implicit in the daughter's rather than the son's caring for a mother, but there may be a painful necessity in this. The dying mother may be comforted by knowing that the person most deeply connected with her is empathizing with her and accompanying her as far as possible on the journey into death. Perhaps in hospitals nurses become surrogate daughters. That is of course a weight for them; but its reward is a deeper connection with the meaning and process of both life and death.

In myth, Hermes was the traditional messenger of death who accompanied the soul to the Underworld. But I think this is a masculine image; women almost never imagine a male as their caretaker or as the messenger of death. It is probably significant, then, that dying Americans most often hallucinate about their mothers. Where the feminine is officially represented (as in godhead of India) but is more demeaned in everyday life, the messenger is usually male and frightening — another example of the masculine bearer of death as cruel and punitive.

THE METAPHYSICS OF GRANDMOTHERING

As we have seen, socially and psychologically there is a fierce sort of individuation in older women. This reflects what Mary Daly calls Crone-ology.[17] But on a metaphysical level, women meet old age and death with a certain acceptance, a quiet knowledge. They embrace beginnings as seen from the perspective of the end of life; the often bitterly gained salt of knowledge helps old women embrace the earth and sea as the elements that will soon surround them in death.

Grandmothering or deepening into the young is one way in which women make the transformative turn toward death. In the first section of Margaret Mead's *Blackberry Winter,* the author portrays her paternal grandmother quietly reigning in the literal center of Mead's parents' home. This woman was central to Mead's development, providing a serene locus and exemplifying feminine individuation in a way that Mead's harried mother was sometimes unable to do. Mead herself discovered the meaning of time and of the last stages of her life in her relationship with her grandchild:

> In the presence of grandparent and grandchild, past and future merge in the present . . . the human unit of time [is] the space between a grandfather's memory of his own childhood and a grandson's knowledge of those memories as he heard about them.
>
> Everyone needs to have access both to grandparents and grandchildren in order to be a full human being.[18]

It is sad to note how Mead falls into a patriarchal reverie, describing time in patrilineal terms even though she traces her own individuation through matrilineal roots, finding an unlooked-for transformation in her bonds with her granddaughter.

The response to grandchildren is not always positive. Tillie Olsen's character Eva, of *Tell Me a Riddle,* recoils from the entrapping flesh of her children's babies because these infants arrest her attempt to contemplate the meaning of her last few days. She knows she is dying of cancer, and they remind her only of her own exhausting and impoverished earlier life stages, spent in mothering too many children. Yet she dies in peace through the care of her adult granddaughter, Jeannie, who quits a nursing job and breaks her engagement to watch over her grandmother. Eva confides her vision of death to Jeannie; Jeannie tells Eva's husband that

> on the last day, she said she would go back to when she first heard music, a little girl on the road of the village where she was born. She promised me. It is a wedding and they dance, while the flutes so joyous and vibrant tremble in the air. Leave her there, Granddaddy, it is all right. She promised me. Come back, come back and help her poor body to die.[19]

This is a profound bequeathal. Eva's granddaughter will carry to her own death this image of an ending that touches its own beginnings.

Few ancient myths about women emanate from the feminine psyche rather than from a masculine experience of the feminine, so Theodora Kroeber's *The Inland Whale* seems especially valuable. Kroeber retells nine California Indian legends that seem to her to be women's fantasies. The title story's quiet power derives from the poignance and love that inform the character and relationships of the protagonist, Nenem. Yet Nenem insists on living alone until the very last stage of her life, when she moves into her son, Toan's, lodge:

> Nenem fitted Pekwoi [the ancestral home where her son now lives] and completed it. She was the grandmother it had been missing. Toan saw how his children liked to be near her. He watched her going up and down the little ladder to the pit and in and out of the low round door, her step smooth and light as always.[20]

Aware of the imminence of her death, Nenem asks to be dressed in a maple-bark skirt and apron like her poverty-stricken mother-in-law, Hune, had worn: she then asks that she be buried next to Hune. Hune had cared for Nenem and her illegitimate son, Toan, for years, while the tribe and Nenem's parents had rejected them. Hune thus gave Nenem the stability of the earth or of the Hestian principle and the containing love that the sea often represents to women. In this tale, the loving sea is embodied as the Inland Whale, an illegitimate child who becomes the spiritual guardian of Nenem and Toan. The whale and the loving mother-in-law are images of the loving matriarchy and natural world that surround Nenem in old age. Like Mead, Nenem learns to understand and accept old age and death through the mediating image of a grandmother, a role that Nenem also takes on.

Intergenerational bonds may be a deeply feminine way of perceiving the passage of time and its meaning. A Jungian analyst and author, Florida Scott-Maxwell, closes *The Measure of My Days* with a loving image of her young grandchild:

> Silence receives too little appreciation, silence being a higher, rarer thing than sound. Silence implies inner riches, and savouring of impressions. Babies value this too . . . My youngest grandchild uses silence as well as he does sound. He is consummate in making soft, confiding noises that bind the heart of the hearer to him. But for long periods he prefers to keep his own counsel . . . He removes his gaze from me so that·I wonder if I was seen, if I was present. With grave deliberation he discovers a hole in the arm of his chair so small that no one else could have had the calm to take it in, and he gives it his undivided attention. He gives all of himself to that hole which just fits the tip of his minute first finger, and I know that all hope of further conversation with him is over. I also know that I have been in the presence of perfect naturalness, and I feel chastened and uplifted.[21]

Ursula LeGuin, one of America's best living writers of science fiction, also writes of grandmothering. In a story called "The Day Before the Revolution," LeGuin features seventy-two-year-old Odo, the founder of a new order, on her last day of life. Childless, Odo confronts the end through images of her own beginnings: she gazes at white-flowered weeds she wandered among as a little girl and muses that she still does not know their names. But the only event in that day that calls forth tears is her love for a young girl, Amai, who helps Odo to dress, "her hair done up by the daughter she had not borne," "so quiet and free and beautiful a child, enough to make you cry when you thought: This is what we worked for, this is what we meant, this is it, here she is, alive, the kindly lonely future."[22] Odo embraces her role as grandmother to the new society, receiving students with affection, but it is Amai, the symbol of her female progeny, who most touches her. It is important to see here that one need not have biological children to become and feel as a grandmother.

Anaïs Nin also demonstrated this propensity for grandmothering in her last years, during which she gathered many young women around her and nurtured their unfolding talents. I was lucky enough to hear the last of her lectures — she knew she was dying and yet only mentioned that this would be her last public appearance — which reflected her kind, patient, affectionate interest in the younger generation. The nurse who cared for Nin in her last days later wrote me a letter, saying that even in pain Nin was caring, considerate, and much concerned with the young women nursing her. Besides her literature, she left us a legacy of affirmation that lasted to her final days. Though she could not give birth herself, she mothered others all her life, sometimes to her detriment.

It may be that nurturing the young gives women the roots to plumb spiritual depths, and helps them to see the rich symbolic meaning of the young. Grandmothering ties a woman to a matrilineal identity that deepens the meaning of birth and death as an ongoing process in which the individual is not lost. She also can see the future potential of her life's work in all the young people who surround her in her old age.

SUICIDE AND OTHER RELINQUISHMENTS OF SELF

Women sometimes enact a pathological maternal embrace that may be part of their suicidal impulses. This seems the negative face of the metaphysical reassurances found in grandmothering. One peculiarly feminine association is the image of a dying young woman fetally curled, sometimes around the bodies of her children. In a natural death, this image reflects a positive closure between a mother and her dead child; for example, in *Tell Me a Riddle,* Tillie Olsen writes that the dying protagonist has carried her dead son's image throughout life and that he will die again with her. But for women who want to die, the image seems to represent a killing of the ability to give life and nurture it. Lily Bart's death in Edith Wharton's *The House of Mirth* gives the fullest sense of this. The day before Lily poisons herself with sedatives, she holds a child:

> Lily felt the soft weight sink trustfully against her breast. The child's confidence in its safety thrilled her with a sense of warmth and returning life . . . as she continued to hold it the weight increased, sinking deeper, and penetrating her with a strange sense of weakness, as though the child entered into her and became a part of herself.

The next day, as she dies,

> the tender pressure of its body was still close to hers: the recovered warmth flowered through her once more, she yielded to it, sank into it, and slept.[23]

The images generated by those who commit suicide also suggest a hope for rebirth—the woman's psyche returns back under and into the earth/sea, but in infant form. This is a common theme in modern fiction by women. Carol Christ has brilliantly developed it in her book *Diving Deep and Surfacing,* where she discusses how Margaret Atwood's *Surfacing* rests on this transformation. The protagonists of Kate Chopin's *The Awakening* and Toni Morrison's *Sula* also die with intimations of their own rebirth. Sula curls in a fetal position, noting with interest the progress of her soul's separation from her body. Her last thoughts are of her best friend Nel: "Well, I'll be damned . . . It didn't even hurt. Wait'll I tell Nel."[24]

Women's pathological attractions to death also reveal a predilection for forms that symbolize a sinking into the mother (drowning) or into the self (drugs or gas fumes). Men are more likely to use mutilating forms of death, leaping from buildings, shooting themselves—obliterating or smashing up the body in an instantaneous destruction of consciousness. Drowning or drugs, the latter especially favored by women, offer a more gradual relinquishing of consciousness. The drowning fantasies of Sylvia Plath and Anne Sexton, for example, reflect the *aqua permanens* (the eternal sea) in its "dangerous, poisonous, primeval state."[25] For these women, water, the Great Mother, must be "submitted to [conjunctive and] transformative processes, before it loses its inflationary and disintegrative properties."[26] Both Plath and Sexton, like Virginia Woolf, rejected living out and through the woundedness of the feminine. Sexton rejected her feminine consciousness and looked for a masculine God; Plath often identified with male artists. Their repressed femininity gained momentous proportions in the unconscious and finally engulfed them, as we see in their water imagery. One of Sexton's last poems is about the "mother ocean"; entitled "The Consecrating Mother," it features the sea as a woman in labor who

> should be entered skin to skin,
> and put on like one's first or last cloth,

entered like kneeling your way into church,
descending into that ascension . . .[27]

To drown during labor is to descend and then to ascend, to be reborn. Plath's last poem is astonishing in its compulsive water imagery:

. . . Water striving
To re-establish its mirror
Over the rock
That drops and turns
A white skull . . .

Words dry and riderless,
The indefatigable hoof-taps
While from the bottom of the pool, fixed stars
Govern a life.[28]

All the poems in Plath's *Ariel* feature water and the Mother Ocean as images of the siren face of death, while consciousness, masculine historicity (the ugliness of words, "white skull") gives way to a sinking to the depths of the pool of fate.

The drowning of Zenobia in Hawthorne's *The Blithedale Romance* is an erroneous masculine idea of what suicide by drowning actually means to a woman. Zenobia drowns herself in a fit of romantic despair; the hook that pulls her from the water pierces her heart. Edna in Chopin's *The Awakening* is also driven by despair to suicide, yet she enters the sea with comfort, consolation, and hope for rebirth. There is nothing violent or mutilating about such suicides; they represent a sinking back into the biological matrix from which life issues. Katherine Ann Porter's "The Jilting of Granny Weatherall" features an image of the extinguishing of the ego: a dying old woman internalizes the flickering candle next to her bedside, makes it symbolic of herself, and then blows it out with her mind as she finally dies. The ego is tiny, quickly engulfed by a larger entity.

Thus, a woman's suicide by drugs, asphyxiation from fumes, or drowning is a gradual loss of consciousness, a sinking away from consciousness. Preserving her body symbolizes the larger female cosmos that will receive and comfort her. The ego rejects its wounds and goes instead into the earth and water of the female unconscious; the transpersonal female body receives the extinguished self. Perhaps this is a mistaken way of achieving the psychological or symbolic ego death that Grof describes. In all these images of a larger watery realm, there is a deep realization of a cosmos into which the consciousness merges, a cosmos that is gigantic, surrounding, perpetually moving and present. Suicidal women like Sexton, Plath, and Woolf are mermaids who refuse the pain of the land-locked life.

In a way, women "die" when they give birth in that they must give up at least some self-development in the public world for the growth and protection of a new person. Even women who continue to work outside of as well as in the home can attest to the energy and time that are taken from their personal lives for the needs of an infant. More than one female writer (especially Anne Sexton) finds the throes of labor and death synonymous.

Both labor and death separate women's psyches from the outside world: to some extent this is also what the paramenstrual stage of women's cycle does. The paramenstrual stage—the days before the onset of their peroids when many women complain of fatigue, irritability, metaphysical gloom—can become a time of contemplation as women turn away from the world and examine their emotions and psyches.

In contrast, a woman's natural death is a fulfilling experience; in the aged woman the sea—death—is quietly immersive and desirable. Actual bodies of water (particularly seawater) and water imagery surround a woman's transformative vision:

> Luna . . . maintains a closer relation to her *prima materia*, the sea, than does Sol; and salt is as it were the crystalline essence which floats in solution in her watery origins . . . Luna, the mother of all things . . . possesses also the healing elixir of life. The wisdom of *aqua permanens*. Thus water and the sea become symbols of the feminine transformative substrata.[29]

The best example of this feminine symbol, for me, is the previously mentioned illegitimate female whale washed into a tiny lake in *The Inland Whale*. This chthonic emissary hears Nenem weeping over her son's future and guides him and Nenem for the rest of their lives. Nenem's own maternal grief connects her to the maternal lovingness of the sea, as embodied in the whale. The whale undergoes a sort of transformation; finally translated into a larger, more comfortable lake, she is released from bondage by her human connections.

In their attitude toward death, then, women show more faith than most men in the cosmos, nature, the Great Mother, that all human consciousness is born out of. If death is the ultimate problem that all religion seeks to resolve, women show great natural faith and affirmation.

II
THE FACES OF MATRIARCHY

When authors write from the depths of their unconscious, raising previously nonverbalized archetypes to consciousness, women's literature can be read as feminine gospel. In this section, I treat both fiction and autobiography. I chose works that emphasize women's confrontation with age and death because this can be the most fruitful time for matriarchal wisdom. Women's old age also needs to be rescued from patriarchal projection; old age in women has been treated as scurrilous, a deliberate attempt on the old women's part to make the feminine principle ugly and sterile. The Elizabethans even coined special language to discuss old women; young women's breasts were called "dainty paps," while old women's were termed "dugs." The emissary of Satan in Spenser's Faerie Queene *is Duessa, an old witch who has no male counterpart in terms of ugliness, age, and evil power.*

In the next chapters, I examine in detail Margaret Laurence's The Stone Angel, *Toni Morrison's* Song of Solomon, *and Colette's* My Mother's House, Sido, The Evening Star, *and* The Blue Lantern. *These works from women of different cultures and family backgrounds give a variety of images of older women; the authors' ages range from early middle age to very old; the works from autobiographical to fiction that is surreal and dreamlike. In a way I see these chapters as a contribution to the growing canon of "Lives of the Saints" for women. Unlike ancient authors on saints, however, these women writers emphasize, rather than erase or gloss over, the flawed humanity of even their most positive characters. They are not impossible role models. Through the close tracing of*

*significant traits of the aged matriarch, the reader will be more
sensitive to imagery that surrounds older women in other works of
art. She can begin to compose her own self-portrait as an older
woman.*

6. Accepting Femininity: Margaret Laurence's *The Stone Angel*

S.E. Read remarks that *The Stone Angel* signals Margaret Laurence's "full maturity as a novelist . . . for here she has created a great central character, untrammeled by bounds of place or time."[1] Hagar, the protagonist, reveals a way of aging and dying that is an important part of the untold story of women's lives.

As I have already mentioned, feminine archetypes until now have been rendered primarily from a male point of view; as central characters, old women have played only a small part in the history of literature. The usual character is like Chaucer's Wife of Bath or Joyce Cary's Sarah Monday—heroines who show that the authors do recognize the energy, strength, and independence of older women, but who also reveal the authors' masculine fears about older women's supposedly voracious sexual appetite. Both these women are picaresque heroines whose lives are defined by a series of sexual episodes, so that what seems like personal autonomy is actually a rapid shifting from one sexual relationship to another. Like chameleons, these characters seem to become whatever anima their men want. Although both have an energetic wit, they never recognize their own essential absurdity, or their lack of completion as beings without male projections. The myopic quality of these characters is further revealed in the fact that neither woman seems ever to contemplate her own death or develop any kind of a metaphysical awareness. Most critics, though not all, see these two female characters as caricatures, which of course renders any religious dimensions unlikely. Chaucer's and Cary's portraits reflect only a type of woman who continues, as always, to serve various male needs. The women intuit what a man finds seductive in women and automatically act that out so as to earn his protection and love. Of course, the women become much more aware of their outer selves, their masks, rather than turning inward for a more introspective and meditative old age. The humor and style of these authors mask a narcissism in their creations which verges on the pathological.

In contrast, Laurence's Hagar is a full and compelling portrait of a different, perhaps antithetical, type of older woman. *The Stone Angel* insists on old age as a time for reverie and reconciliation with all that has gone before. Hagar's whole life is in essence her old age, because it is then that she finally comes to terms with her life pattern, reconciles it, and finally transcends its limitations. Her strengths help her to forge a transformation out of an often bitter past. The novel argues that women have the free will to make attitudinal changes, even in a life that seems to have been almost entirely determined by external factors.

The Stone Angel is one of the four novels of the Manawaka series that Margaret Laurence bases on her girlhood home of Manitoba, Canada. Each novel features a different heroine based on one of the elements: earth, air, fire, or water; Hagar is the earth element. She is the daughter of one of Manawaka's founding patriarchs, but marries a poor farmer and ends up selling eggs to women whom she considers beneath her. The entire novel is stream-of-consciousness as Hagar complains about being an ailing and elderly widow residing with her only surviving son, Marvin, and his gentle, rather martyred wife, Doris, both of whom Hagar compares unfavorably to her dead son, John, and her own proud and ruthless younger self. The novel centers around Hagar's escape from a rest home where she has been taken because of her increasing incontinence and forgetfulness. She escapes to an old cannery beside the sea and tells many stories of her past to a stranger who finds her there. In turning over the past, she lets go of her pride and accepts love for her husband, Bram, whom she had rejected as socially beneath her. She also finally accepts Marvin and Doris in an act that signals growth out of the rigid set of values she has lived.

THE ABSENCE OF THE FOUNDING MOTHER
IN HAGAR'S CHILDHOOD

One of the first things to notice about Hagar is that she lacks the strong, deep matrilineal roots which are crucial for an older woman who is trying to resolve and understand her life pattern. Hagar's psychic rigidity, her inflexible pride, can be traced directly to the absence of a positive feminine influence in her childhood. Indeed, she is bereft of almost all feminine influence. Her mother dies at her birth; she has no sisters, or grandmother, only an aunt who favors Hagar's brother Dan. Aunt Dolly is a weak figure, and very homely with her "sallow skin" and "top incisors that protruded like a jack rabbit,"[2] so that she usually covers her face with her hand when she talks—an image of self-abnegation with which the young, smart, and energetic Hagar could scarcely wish to identify. Hagar is further shamed by her father, who wishes out loud that she were a boy since she is smarter and stronger than his two sons.

Furthermore, Hagar's brothers' lives warn her away from any "soft" feminine attributes. Dan is sensitive and sickly, and Matt is gentle, a thinker. The father's critical and proud harshness serves to drive Matt further into himself and to harden Hagar against the softness that Matt embodies. A wounded and hurt child, Dan dies; Matt also dies, as an adult, in a passive, receptive, way. Thus, Hagar early learns that survival means a rejection of all the positive aspects of the feminine principle, such as tenderness, gentleness, openness, flexibility.

Although her brothers embody some of these traits, they further the process by which Hagar is hardened against trusting (or really loving) anyone by beating her whenever their father beats them. Hagar's childhood, therefore, is not only desolate of love, but is a chain of cruelty. Hagar internalizes her father's masculine pride and his unconscious hatred of all the good things the feminine principle can stand for, and learns that the harshest of masculine values lead to survival.

HAGAR AS A DEVOURING MOTHER

As an adult, Hagar embodies a pattern familiar in literature— women who reject their feminine role yet cannot act out their masculine, aggressive side because of cultural taboos, and who thus seek a male delegate to act for them. Lady Macbeth and Volumnia,

Coriolanus's mother, are two such figures in Shakespeare's works. Like Volumnia, Hagar can see her sons only in terms of how well they will compete—reflect her—in the world; she is unable to nurture the men in her home with a feminine disinterest that loves and accepts family members and shapes the innate material of her children's selves to the highest form it can take for their own sake. It is important to see that Hagar is bereft of women once again—she has only sons.

Among the most poignant moments in the book are those when the young Marvin stands mutely in front of his mother after telling her he has done his chores (and often his drunken father's, too). The only thing this child is able to do to win his mother's love is to work hard; his longing for her praise and recognition throughout his life is a muted suffering, as he is the sort of person who cannot speak of his pain. Perhaps this reflects Hagar's own inability to speak of her pain; she denies her grief and needs for almost her whole life. But instead of responding to Marvin, Hagar focuses on her other son, John, in hope that he will fulfill her great expectations and help her to better her prestigious father.

A contemptuous wife and a mercilessly demanding mother, Hagar contributes much to the forces that destroy her husband and John. The death of John and Arlene, his fiancée, reflects the terrible image of the dead Royal Couple, ordinarily an archetype of wholeness, balance, and futurity. When the two who embody this image die, both sets of parents undergo excruciating grief and guilt. Their own futures and hopes are annihilated in their children's deaths. There is no one left who is worthy to carry Hagar's fantasies, or so she feels. Yet she holds in the pain of this image for many years, not confronting her grief until her last days.

THE ROOTS OF HAGAR'S PAIN AND STRENGTH

It seems to me that Hagar's lifelong psychic dilemma deserves more compassion than most critics give it. The turning point in Hagar's awareness comes in the following oft-quoted passage:

> Pride was my wilderness, and the demon that led me there was fear. I was alone, never anything else, and never free, for I carried my chains within me, and they spread out from me and shackled all I touched. Oh, my two, my dead. Dead by your own hands or by mine? Nothing can take away those years.[3]

All critics see pride as central to Hagar's character, but no one has written much about the separation and fear that her life has embodied. Her isolation from matrilineal connections, her lack of feminine roots, underlies the fear and loneliness that cause her pride. She has no mother, sisters, daughters — not even a friend. Hagar is bound by the most pathological and polarizing phase of the Oedipus complex, denying the feminine and identifying herself only with the masculine. She is unable to relate in depth with anyone because of her rejection of the feminine ability to accept others as complete and right in themselves. She is thus always terribly alone but has never had any standard of closeness through which she can understand this. The more permeable ego membrane that a daughter develops in relationship to her mother never does become part of Hagar, even in the resolution of the novel, when she does finally manage to find her way into a deeper connection with her daughter-in-law and her granddaughter.

Yet there are innate forces in Hagar that surge finally against the walls she has built around herself. Her craggy strength and ferocious wit keep the reader from pitying her and form the base of the psychological and intellectual strength that lead to her eventual transformation. Maturity and multiple perspective merge into a sense of irony. She is able to see that even in her best lilac dress, she cuts a rather grotesque figure. Unfortunately, she also uses her savage humor as part of a defense against the strongest embodiment of the protective, nurturing Demeter phase of womanhood that she ever has known in her life, her daughter-in-law, Doris.

HAGAR'S RE-MEMBERING OF HER MATRILINEAL ROOTS

Hagar's acceptance of the feminine catalyzes and consolidates her final transformation. Late in the novel, this is symbolized by her visit to the cemetery. Marvin, Doris, and Hagar stop at the grave of Hagar's mother, whose headstone bears a stone angel; Hagar sees that Bram's people have been buried close to hers in a symbolic gathering together of the founding families. Hagar realizes that both families are founding families and that later generations do not see one as superior to the other, as her father did; the elderly Hagar sees this as right and true: "That was as it should be."[4] She gives up the either/or patriarchal patterns of thought for the both/and, more matriarchal way of thinking. Hagar also eventually realizes her essential kinship with her girlhood rival, Lottie, as she remembers how they plotted against their children's marriage: "There we sat, among the doilies and the teacups, two fat old women, no longer haggling with one another, but only with fate, pitting our wits against God's."[5] Lottie becomes the missing sister in Hagar's life, although Hagar only fully accepts her in her memories.

Before Hagar can reflect her new sense of the feminine, she goes to the sea and confronts the shadow figure of her own masculine principle, Murray Lees. Lees, like Hagar, has been carrying on patrilineal rigidity, pride, and piety; like Hagar, he is a bereft parent whose child is an indirect victim of Lee's negative masculine traits. The two drink wine together—a sort of Dionysian communion and confession—and finally Hagar cries, for the first time in her life, about John. The imagery preceding this scene, when Hagar descends many stairs, reflects her "transcending downward," away from Apollonian light to darkness and water, an ameliorated and softened animus figure who readies her for her much needed union with the feminine principle.

When Hagar at last enters the hospital, she learns to feel sisterhood links with the other dying old women in her ward, although she earlier calls them "unanimous old ewes" or "hens." By the time Marvin moves her out of the ward she regrets her complaints, and in her new ward she demonstrates her acceptance of her Demeter roots in a relationship with her roommate, Sandra, who at first seems very alien to her. Recall that older women often describe themselves in terms of very old, deeply rooted, sheltering trees. Invoking this image, Hagar says that Sandra is "green and slender, a sapling of a girl."[6]

Hagar's personal growth and redemption, however, is signaled most in her sudden awareness of a matrilineal alliance with her daughter-in-law, Doris. Doris is startled, taken aback when Hagar tugs off her family ring and gives it to Doris to give to Tina, the granddaughter. Hagar wishes she had given it to Doris earlier. Doris is the last figure we see in the novel, standing beside Hagar and giving Hagar a cup of water, which symbolizes more than the communion cup that some critics name it. The water represents feminine relatedness, which Hagar takes from Doris, admitting her need and accepting the balm. For Hagar, Doris embodies many faces of the feminine: wife, mother, and caring sister. The reader has always seen Doris as containing, nurturing, even pampering

Hagar, making her favorite cake and giving her the best slices of roast beef, caring for her during the night, changing wet sheets — and all this in spite of Doris's own failing heart (an irony, in that she has more heart than anyone else in Hagar's life). Hagar finally accepts Doris as her closest ally. She leaves the family of her father and, with the ring that she gives Doris, symbolically enters into her daughter-in-law's line. The acknowledgement of this tie is a heroic step in consciousness.

HAGAR'S FEMININE METAPHYSICS

It is important to see that Laurence gifts her protagonist with a metaphysics that is firmly grounded in her own feminine experience. Hagar emphatically rejects the patriarchal Christian point of view she has been taught, subjecting Doris's minister, Mr. Troy, to a sound vocal drubbing whenever he approaches her. She rejects the masculine images of heaven as inorganic and static, saying she likes this life:

> How I shall hate to go away for good.
> Even if heaven were real, and measured as Revelation says, so many cubits this way and that, how gimcrack a place it would be, crammed with its pavements of gold, its gates of pearl and topaz, like a gigantic chunk of costume jewelry. Saint John of Patmos can keep his sequined heaven, or share it with Mr. Troy, for all I care, and spend eternity in fingering the gems and telling each other gleefully they're worth a fortune.[7]

We are prepared for her own final insight through earlier imagery, when Hagar claims knowledge of birth that Doris does not have:

> If she's ever had to take their [calves] wet half-born heads and help draw them out of the mother, she might call them by many words, but *sweet* would almost certainly not be one of them. And yet it's true I always had some feeling for any creature struggling awkward and unknowing into life.[8]

She has feminine knowledge of spheres of reality that supports her as she dies:

> When my second son was born, he found it difficult to breathe at first. He gasped a little, coming into the unfamiliar air. He couldn't have known before or suspected at all that breathing would be what was

done by creatures here. Perhaps the same occurs elsewhere, an element
so unknown you'd never suspect it at all.[9]

She sees that birth is perhaps like death, in that it seems to the infant
an ending and yet is in reality a beginning. She implicitly sees a
correspondence between the spiritual and natural spheres.
Laurence's conscious presentation of the image of birth as a
feminine premonition of immortality is an important aspect of *The
Stone Angel*.

Many of Hagar's characteristics present a different picture of
older women from that created by male writers. First, though men
have been important to her life, she has no need for the erotic in her
old age. She seems to have been a one-man woman; after Bram dies,
she never connects with another man. Second, she never leaves her
children behind as though they were only part of a previous stage in
life, and she never stops learning from them. Third, Laurence spares
us none of the terrible facts of old age; Hagar's physical problems
are described in all their painful grotesqueness, yet her internal
appreciation of nature and life is splendid, lovely. Fourth, Hagar's
metaphysics are profoundly her own, rooted in her own life
experiences; she is a meditative, reflective old woman. Fifth,
Laurence shows that the possibility for epiphany, for transformation, exists until the very last moment of life; *The Stone Angel*
is an affirmation of old age and dying as a time for discovering
meaning and for final reckonings.

Women's need for other women is also emphasized in Hagar's
transformation. Her connection with the feminine, the matrilineal,
is crucial to her final steps of individuation and transformation.
Although her rejection of the feminine principle throughout her life
has been as adamant as any man's could be, she connects finally
with other old women, her young roommate, her daughter-in-law,
her granddaughter, and the feminine principle of water. These are
only external connections; her intrapsychic connections with her
friends and her family also help transform her.

Finally, Hagar seems to be the most fully developed older-woman
character that we have so far. She is perhaps at an opposite pole
from Virginia Woolf's Mrs. Dalloway and Mrs. Ramsey, who, at
one with the feminine principle and values, embody less troubled,
lifelong, tender maternal containment and familial connections.
Hagar, in some ways more interesting, reminds me of Lillian

Hellman, or of Hilary Stevens in May Sarton's *Mrs. Stevens Hears the Mermaids Singing*, or of Maya Angelou's grandmother in *I Know Why the Caged Bird Sings*, or of Maxine Hong Kingston's mother in *Woman Warrior*. Like Hagar, such women individuate more powerfully because of the strength they develop in fighting against restrictions.

We can apply many names to Hagar's embodiment of this feminine archetype. Northrup Frye says Canadian consciousness rests on an image of the land as an "unseizable virginity."[10] Hagar seems to draw much of her ferocity and her compulsion toward individuation from her identification with the land, which for most Canadian women writers is represented as an ally, not an antagonist. Mary Daly's new definition of crone perhaps best reflects Hagar's Canadian brand of tough, sinewy, craggy consciousness: "A woman becomes a Crone as a result of Surviving early stages of the Otherworld Journey and therefore having discovered depths of courage, strength, and wisdom in herself."[11] Hagar has survived a long and difficult sojourn in the loneliest of patriarchal domains, both within and without. In her last days she finds the strength and courage to forge new wisdom. Buffeted by the winds of her time and culture, she grows crooked; not all the young under her branches survive, but she does grow — somewhat gnarled, sometimes yielding bitter fruit, but with enormous and indefatigable strength. Hagar: the chthonic forces, strong and unfurled to the winds.

7. Femininity as Entrapment: The Older Woman in Toni Morrison's *Song of Solomon*

Probably fewer women are fixated in the patterns elucidated in Chapter VI than are those who suffer from the opposite kind of limitation. Many women live out the first and sometimes the second half of life completely and only immersed in matriarchal structure and values. They do not reach their full unfolding because they have been cut off from meaningful, trustworthy relationships with either men or positive masculine values. Women can develop in two opposite ways if they are cut off from the masculine principle. Morrison's *Song of Solomon* portrays these ways.

Song of Solomon embraces four generations, although most of the novel takes place during the protagonist, Milkman's, mid-thirties. Milkman lives with his parents, Macon and Ruth, but his aunt Pilate, who lives with her daughter, Reba, and granddaughter, Hagar, provides another kind of home for him. Milkman owes his life to Pilate, who returned to town when Macon had refused for years to sleep with Ruth because of what he perceived as her incestuous longing for her dead father. Pilate put a charm on her brother, and he impregnated Ruth with Milkman. Milkman further owes his first sexual experience and long love affair to his cousin Hagar, always available to him at Pilate's house. He ultimately rejects Hagar, who by this time is in her late thirties, and she commits suicide. Milkman then makes a journey south in search of gold, but he really finds his own roots and selfhood. Pilate accompanies him on this journey and buries her father's bones on his land, long ago stolen by white people. In the end, Milkman's friend Guitar, aiming to kill Milkman for his gold, shoots and kills Pilate.

Milkman is Morrison's *intended* protagonist, but Pilate slips out of her grasp into greater magnitude than Milkman; readers, both men and women, remember Pilate in much more detail and more powerfully than they do Milkman. Hawthorne had not intended for Zenobia or Hester to become main characters in his novels, either; for both Morrison and Hawthorne, these characters suggest the power of feminine archetypes. Just as one remembers Hester long after Dimmsdale's name is forgotten, so Pilate is a far more numinous, original, and vivid character than Milkman is.

The matriarchal image is expanded and brought fully to life in *Song of Solomon*. Pilate extends Morrison's earlier characters, yet Pilate as the cultural matriarch and Circe, another character, as the priestess healer interpenetrate more than in the previous novels. These characters also move more powerfully and surely into both the foreground, as fully realized characters, and the background, as the feminine ground of being on which many of the other characters consciously and unconsciously depend and out of which they evolve.

There are three old women in this novel—Circe and Ruth as important but less affirmative personalities, and Pilate as the alternative archetype. The character of Circe is based on a literal enslavement of a woman to a house. Morrison has spoken in another context about the psychological significance of a woman's relationship to her house:

> I think 'Song' is more expansive . . . I had to loosen up. I could not create the same kind of enclosed world that I had in previous books. Before it was as if I went into a room and shut the door in my books. I tried to pull the reader into that room. But I couldn't do that with Milkman. It's a feminine concept—things happening in a room, a house. That's where we live, in houses. Men don't live in those houses, they really don't. My ex-husband is an architect and he didn't live there: every house is a hotel to him. [1]

To many of Morrison's women, their houses are integral psychological forces, structures that limit and define their very beings. Morrison encapsulates in Circe the most entrapped and bitter relationship between a woman and a house in perhaps all of literature. The twisted and archetypal depths of this figure are extraordinary. She becomes a Hestia turned sour, a Sophia/Fury, pure salt and earth, no water. She is a black version of the Roman Vestal Virgin, sentenced forever to slave for the collective. She is the house's digestive system.

Circe represents the climactic development of the witch priestess in Morrison's fiction. She is a midwife and, as Milkman says, "Healer, deliverer, in another world she would have been the head nurse at Mercy."[2] Like Homer's Circe, she gives a map to Milkman, the young questing male, directing him to his nemesis. She surrounds herself with a pack of dreadful dogs which seem to be the final metamorphosis of the white family she served for so many generations. She is ageless, apparently about two hundred years old, yet she has the voice of a young girl, and when she first embraces Milkman, he has an erection. Morrison alludes to the witch in Hansel and Gretel as Milkman nears Circe's house; he senses her power over birth, life, and death in the crawling vegetation and odors of death and spices in the house itself. She stands at the top of a staircase as he enters her decaying mansion. Like all Morrison's witch women, she towers over him.

She is also a deliverer. She saves Macon and Pilate from being killed by hiding them in the attic of the Butlers' house. Yet with all her spiritual and intellectual strength, which manifests itself in her salty tongue, she has been immured in that house by a gradually dying out white aristocratic family. She has been forced into a Hestian role that becomes one-sided, and hence monomaniacal. Her midwifery seems linked to the Butlers' barrenness. Fittingly, she participates in everyone else's fertility, but brings the Butlers none. The most degrading image of all for her is when the last living Butler woman kills herself rather than have to participate in the drudgery that Circe is immersed in every day. As Circe tells Milkman,

> "She killed herself rather than do the work I'd been doing all my life! . . . Do you hear me? She saw the work I did all her days and *died*, you hear me, *died* rather than live like me. Now, what do you suppose she thought I was! If the way I lived and the work I did was so hateful to her she killed herself to keep from having to do it, and you think I stay on here because I loved her, then you have about as much sense as a fart!"[3]

Forced into one feminine role, she has become all that Hestia represses, the demonic and destructive Hestian; she stays in the house and presides over its demise by dirt, rot, damage, lack of care, and the deliberate tearing apart by the dogs. Rather than turn nature to culture, she changes culture to refuse, to excrement. She is in the last livable room as she talks to Milkman. For Circe the house is the body of her white mistress; it is ravished, torn asunder by the dogs who will do likewise to Circe, the last human linked to their dynasty, when she finally falls dead among them. She especially delights in telling Milkman about the destruction in the house:

> "I will never clean it again. Never. Nothing. Not a speck of dust, not a grain of dirt, will I move. Everything in this world they lived for will crumble and rot. The chandelier already fell down and smashed itself to pieces. It's down there in the ballroom now. All in pieces. Something gnawed through the cords. Ha! And I want to see it all go, make sure it does go, and that nobody fixes it up. I brought the dogs in to make sure . . . You ought to see what they did to her bedroom. Her walls didn't have wallpaper. No. Silk brocade that took some Belgian women six years to make. She loved it — oh, how much she loved it. Took thirty Weimaraners one day to rip it off the walls. If I thought the stink wouldn't strangle you, I'd show it to you."[4]

Circe's dogs are fearfully sinister. They hum, and as Circe delivers this liturgy, they hum louder, one sitting on each side of her as if she were the Queen of Egypt with a sphinx on each side of her throne. The humming suggests a beehive; she has become the queen bee who shuts down the hive and will be eaten by her own drones. Like the aged Eva in the last sequence of Morrison's earlier novel *Sula*, this eldest of all the crones and furies has become mad, but rationally so, against the backdrop of an insane and killing world. What has been done to Circe is terrible (again like Eva), but what she has become in spite of it all is strange and wondrous. She renders the true spirit of the white aristocracy, uncovering its rottenness, filth, and sterility, its bestiality. And she helps Milkman as she helped Pilate and Macon. She is a life-giving Demeter to the good and needy; she has only lost one woman among those babies she delivered, and that was Pilate's mother. Circe is a demonic yet truth-telling and life-giving Sophia, her strength and wisdom finally formidable. She is the most magical, terrifying, and perhaps cosmic of all Morrison's characters.

A doctor's daughter and a rich man's wife, Ruth Macon is the social antithesis of Circe, yet her relationship to her house also underlies the despair and hopelessness she feels about her life. Her house is a force, a character against which she must define herself. It is important to understand Ruth's dilemma because we see then how crucial Pilate is to Ruth's redemption and final individuation. At the end of the novel, Ruth is sixty-four, and Pilate, sixty-eight, is her final and highest mentor, her Wise Old Woman archetype.

Pitifully isolated from birth, Ruth lived her whole life in her father's house. She is her "daddy's daughter," a *puella*, not a Persephone.[5] Her mother died when she was born and she grew up deeply attached to her father, investing her adolescent adoration with the sexuality of an adult woman. She does not see herself as incestuous, but Macon and the reader, to a lesser degree, do. If Macon had been a different man, she could have transferred all that animus energy from her father to Macon and grown up. But Macon psychologically bludgeons her whenever she shows any individuality or initiative, such as creating centerpieces for the table. She tells her son, Milkman, finally that she knows she is a small person, but that she has been pressed small.

In relationship to her home, Ruth is a failed Demeter, an inverse Hestia. She has been unable to mother her daughters into normal male/female relationships; even when she tries to "cultivate small life" like fish or plants, they die. In Hestian terms, she cannot manage the process of her home. Her cooking is always terrible; her Christmas trees are ugly, anti-festive; and no one feels contained or comforted in the house. Her daughters feel imprisoned; her son and husband feel surrounded by sterility. The only thing in the house with which she senses connection is the flower bowl that her status-seeking father featured in their home. Her husband rejects her sexually and she lives untouched by a man from age twenty, except for the few days when Pilate bewitches Macon into desiring Ruth so that Milkman is conceived.

When Pilate arrives in town to assist Ruth in conceiving her last child, she essentially saves Ruth's life. Except for visits to the grave of her father, who becomes an unattainable Hades figure, making her long for death, Ruth's only human anchor of love is Pilate. It is on Pilate's behalf that Ruth finally stands up to Macon in one of the fiercest moments of the novel. When Hagar commits suicide, Ruth's feminine alliance with Pilate surfaces:

It was touch and go whether she'd have a decent funeral until Ruth walked down to Sonny's Shop and stared at Macon without blinking. He reached into his cash drawer and pulled out two twenty-dollar bills and put them down on the desk. Ruth didn't stretch out her hand to pick them up, or even shift her feet. Macon hesitated, then wheeled around in his chair and began fiddling with the combination to his safe. Ruth waited. Macon dipped into the safe three separate times before Ruth unclasped her hands and reached for the money. "Thank you," she said, and marched off to Linden Chapel Funeral Home to make the fastest arrangements possible.[6]

Ruth not only loved Pilate for what she had done for her but also loved her for herself. Particularly in the phrase "stared at Macon without blinking" do we see a ferocity that probably surprises Ruth herself. This rich, pampered, "almost white" doctor's daughter finds her own feminine soul image in Pilate. She becomes finally a strong mother figure, a Demeter through alliance with Pilate. Milkman makes this connection between the two women, raising them both to a single figure of the Demeter/Sophia:

With two exceptions, everybody he was close to seemed to prefer him out of this life. And the two exceptions were both women, both black, both old. From the beginning, his mother and Pilate had fought for his life, and he had never so much as made either of them a cup of tea.[7]

Milkman senses the deep link and bond between these two women. Ruth remains entrapped in Macon's and her father's house, in her daughter/wife roles, but she abides and grows anyway — through Pilate. The importance of women to each other for consolidation of the soul, for last stages of metaphysical growth, is emphasized by Morrison. In spite of all that Macon and her father did to stunt her growth, Ruth manages enough individuation by the end of this novel that one cannot but like her, congratulate her.

Pilate's entry into the world establishes her independence, and this autonomy she partially teaches Ruth. Pilate too defines herself through feminine values and roles, but not in relationship to patriarchal definitions. She is cut off early from human culture, so she can choose what she wants as she makes her own world. Circe tells Milkman that Pilate gave birth to herself, her mother dying before delivery and Pilate wriggling out anyway after everyone presumed the baby dead. Her mysterious lack of a navel further supports and enforces her psychic rebirth when again she midwives herself. She has no choice but to become a loner, to care for herself. She is isolated and rejected.

> When she realized that she would always be alone, she threw away every assumption she had learned and began at zero. First off, she cut her hair. That was one thing she didn't want to have to think about anymore. Then she tackled the problem of trying to decide how she wanted to live and what was valuable to her. When am I happy and when am I sad and what is the difference? What do I need to know to stay alive? What is true in the world? . . . since death held no terrors for her (she often spoke to the dead), she knew there was nothing to fear.[8]

> She gave up, apparently, all interest in table manners or hygiene, but acquired a deep concern for and about human relationships . . . She was a natural healer, and among quarreling drunks and fighting women she could hold her own, and sometimes mediated a peace that lasted a good bit longer than it should have because it was administered by someone not like them.[9]

Her path is truly the path of Tao, the path that responds to life's deepest spiritual concerns because the traveler has exorcised the driving ego forces of fear and ambition.[10] The external world no longer determines her character. Except for her love of nature as a child, the external world never has much impact on Pilate; when she consciously and deliberately turns to her own values, human bonds become her study and concern. Pilate embodies the selfless life of pure *eros*, of total receptiveness to life, that Milkman will eventually understand and embrace.

Pilate is perhaps the most majestic and regal of all old women in literature. Her sensitive, mobile, chewing mouth suggests her constant mental and spiritual cogitation on all that passes before her. Her protection of Ruth and Milkman from her own brother shows her concern for the frail and vulnerable in the world. When a man attacks Reba, Pilate's daughter, Pilate shoves a knife to his throat. As she does this, an earring in her left earlobe flashes heroically. Her earring, a small metal box that contains her name (the only word her father ever wrote), flashes also at Hagar's funeral as her anger again flows out. She wears the earring in her left earlobe, emphasizing her matriarchal consciousness which protects her daughter and granddaughter as well as Milkman and Ruth. (The left side of the body has always been associated with the feminine, the *yin*. Remember that John Milton in *Paradise Lost* portrays Eve as created from a rib from Adam's left side; his weaker feminine side produces the less rational and moral Eve.)

Like all of Morrison's old and spiritually powerful women, Pilate looms large to those around her. Milkman is astonished at her height; her black dress, a quilt instead of a coat, and unlaced shoes become the apparel of a queen. While Circe can change white people to dogs, Pilate can metamorphose herself. In the police station she becomes an Aunt Jemima, shrinking small and speaking in dialect in order to get Milkman out of jail. In the car on the way home from jail, with Macon driving, Milkman notices she has grown tall again; her head, now wrapped in silk, is touching the top of the car. Her language returns to its crystalline and eloquent purity. When fully aroused, she becomes a bull elephant; listen to how she ends Hagar's funeral:

> Suddenly, like an elephant who had just found his anger and lifts his trunk over the heads of the little men who want his teeth or his hide or his flesh or his amazing strength, Pilate trumpeted for the sky itself to hear, "And she was *loved*!"[11]

Pilate's favorite reading is an old geography book; this restlessness and her chameleon cunning suggest the tricky and adventurous Hermes. This archetype often surfaces in descriptions of old women, because they manifest the masculine elements of fire, air, and sulfur — elements of ferocity and strength that make their anger a force that moves others.

Yet she is as abiding as the earth and as stable in her way as Eva in *Sula*. She is the Hestian, Demeter, containing principle of woman for those who depend upon her. Her father liked the way her name looked, thinking the capital letter was sheltering those other letters like a tall tree. Pilate's size, her protective energy, her intelligence and selfless devotion suggest the intimate protection of the larger for the smaller. Milkman is happy in a domestic setting for the first time in his life when he visits Pilate's house. Pilate's interest in Milkman as an infant and as an adult reflects probably some unconscious hunger in her for a male relative, but one never senses that she needs him for her own individuation process. On the other hand, he does take her to her childhood home so she can bury her daddy's bones, although for her the trip is fatal. His reciprocation is thus ambivalent, but it does exist.

Perhaps Pilate's individuation is full and her whole life mobile because she spent her girlhood with a loving father and brother. As an adult woman she contends with the negative animus values of her brother and consistently wins. She also plays surrogate mother to Milkman, who carries her with him in his epic journey south in search of their roots. Thus Pilate has some very early animus connections to real men that help carry her individuation further than it might have gone.

Pilate's spiritual gifts are her most magnificent bequest to Milkman and so to us. She is brilliantly meditative on the different colors and textures of black and on the process of cooking a perfect soft-boiled egg. The first time he visits her, Pilate gives Milkman his first perfect egg.[12] The same day she shows him the color blue so that he really sees it; blue, of course, reflects infinite spirituality. The perfection of the egg and her love of blue merge into a jewel-like but natural image; it is as if she gives him communion but in a feminine sense. She also finally teaches Milkman spiritual responsibility; she carries the bones of a man she believed she helped kill, and she saves the dead Hagar's hair for Milkman. She teaches him that you must carry your own sins, your betrayals of others, in order to gain a soul. Thus she helps with Ruth's conceiving of Milkman, protects Ruth's pregnancy from Macon, and then acts as midwife to Milkman's soul.

She goes south with him in utter regality to put her father's bones to rest. Recovered from Hagar's death, she wears a mink stole that Reba had won, and "peace circled her."[13] There is a jubilance in Pilate that is part of her life force and that resurfaces in spite of the loss of Hagar. Morrison says she has always sensed a greater joy and love of life in black women than in black men;[14] she builds this element into Pilate as a powerful force for good and for ongoingness. Pilate thinks her father has commanded her to sing, and it is in her to follow such a dictate of celebration in spite of all life's miseries. When Guitar shoots her in the closing scene of the novel, her first words are for another: "Watch Reba for me." Then she gives Milkman her last lesson and it is the essence of *caritas*: "I wish I'd a knowed more people. I would of loved 'em all. If I'd a knowed more, I would a loved more."[15] Milkman sings to her, and when she dies, a bird whirls down and flies into the sky with her earring, surely an allusion to the epic tradition of bird signs as the word of God. Milkman's real epiphany comes at Pilate's death:

> Now he knew why he loved her so. Without ever leaving the ground, she could fly. "There must be another one like you," he whispered to her. "There's got to be at least one more woman like you."[16]

Pilate never leaves the ground though she can fly, which is unlike the males of this and other novels by Morrison; men fly off and abandon their wives and children, but though Pilate knew the value of roaming and loved to roam, she always took care of her dependents. She never flew ungrounded in love. Milkman leaps to his death fight with Guitar knowing that "if you surrendered to the air, you could *ride* it"; in other words, he has opened himself to life in the same selfless, intense way that Pilate has. He has internalized the relatedness, the *eros*, the spirituality of this magnificent old woman; his flying will be grounded in the compassion and stern strength of this woman who embodied such a highly developed and uniquely individual feminine principle.

An important image in Morrison's depictions of old women is the tree, which suggests a natural and rooted Demeter strength. The masculine-generated archetype of marriage features women as vines, needing the strength of the male tree;[17] the frail vine brings beauty and fertility to the tree in exchange for its support. This may be true for the earliest stage of many marriages, when women have small children and need the protective shelter of a home and man. But older women often identify with trees, and even younger women writers often present this image.[18] It is interesting to note here that Milkman's sister Lena had a tree that took root and grew from Milkman's urinating on it, but it finally died. The tree as a woman's self must be rooted in soil of her own choosing.

Remember that Pilate's father intuitively grasped the essence of her being in his choice of a name that looks like a sheltering tree. Milkman, the character who by the end of the novel most nearly matches her complexity and depth, perceives her as a tree when, as a boy, he first sees her: he is astonished by the numinosity "of this lady who had one earring, no navel, and looked like a tall black tree."[19] This image of a tree further emphasizes the sheltering, ferociously protective quality of Pilate, who does what she can, always, to protect weaker, more dependent people than herself. Pilate's name is a real irony as she has the deepest integrity of anyone in the novel, can always be counted on, would never betray anyone (as did the Biblical Pilate). Macon, of course, feels she has betrayed his middle-class values, but his point of view on Pilate only shows how little he can perceive authenticity. He cannot sense the depth of her roots or the sheltering quality of her branches.

I do not mean to imply that Pilate's patterns of living have not cost something. In three of her novels, Morrison expresses the inability to grow, the psyche turning back on itself, as incest longing. An attempt to literalize the intrapsychic longing to give up the heroic struggle for self in the world beyond the family always turns out to be fatal. In Morrison's *The Bluest Eye*, Pecola's father impregnates her with a child that dies shortly after birth; thereafter the family and its individual members disintegrate. Pecola and her mother live on, a barren and mad image of the mother/daughter, Demeter/Persephone archetype. In *Sula*, Plum longs to re-enter the swaddled comfort of the mother body; he is the first of her children that Eva must kill. In *Song of Solomon*, the motherless Ruth confuses her erotic longings at adolescence with her love for her father; Macon senses her incestuous desire and permanently rejects her. Ruth's daughters, in turn, are like Persephone, caught in the underworld by Macon, a cruel Hades who renders them barren.

But Hagar is the real casualty of incest longing in *Song of Solomon*. Pilate tells her that Milkman is like her brother, yet Hagar has grown up in a world with no rules, no taboos, no father figure, which is perhaps a girl's first introduction to the incest taboo. She has grown up in a totally sheltered and feminine world and does not understand how grown women individuate vis-à-vis grown men. She has lived in a separatist world. In a sense she never leaves the mother body, because even her one sexual relationship is with a cousin/brother. Pilate's total sheltering of this child keeps her just that. Hagar never enters into the first stages of adulthood; at age thirty-six she is still feverishly trying to establish herself as an adult woman with a permanent relationship outside her family. She should be contemplating the advent of middle age, but she still has the mind of a young girl.

Reba is a muted figure who also fails to individuate, at least partially because of Pilate. Reba gives everything away to men, relies on her innate good luck (feminine intuition as the only and hence irrational mode of acting), is protected by her mother, and remains always childlike. Reba's "simplicity might also be vacuousness" and she has "the simple eyes of an infant."[20] Morrison never tells us Reba's age, as if it is an irrelevant fact.

But one must not blame Pilate for these results of her matriarchal realm. What choice had she? Like Eva of *Sula*, Pilate had to rely only on her own strength and wisdom. No one ever gives anything to her; she must even give birth to herself. It may be significant that each of Morrison's novels becomes fuller and richer as the older women gain more individuation, more scope, and become more central. Perhaps one of the deepest epiphanies for a woman is her learning what the last stage of life can hold for her; for a younger woman, like Morrison, this comes through a deep appreciation of older women. *Song of Solomon* is basically an epic, but unlike male-authored epics such as Ellison's *Invisible Man*, the women are not mere signposts on the hero's trip. Pilate roves the United States for years before seeing that Ruth needs her and that Hagar needs the roots of place and kin. Women can be movers and wanderers in Morrison's world. In some ways one could say that these characters represent one version of a very American value—Emersonian self-reliance. They go it alone: without benefit of clergy, welfare, marriage, help from any man, these women become queens in their own domains. And they become images of possibility, archetypes of futurity. Their old age is an accomplishment, a richness, a diversity of self. They demonstrate the metaphysical strengths women can find in themselves. These old women are neo-Renaissance women: weathered embodiments of active and contemplative virtue at the service of their culture.

8. Matriarch as Tender Ferocity: Colette

Colette was a great matriarch, a woman born ahead of her time. It is only recently that we have begun to appreciate Colette's career and her lifelong devotion to the world of women. Yet her development and life pattern were in most ways antithetical to those of the older women presented in earlier chapters. Laurence's and Morrison's matriarchs individuate in spite of an almost total lack of support systems. They have no positive loving relationships with men; worse, they are bereft of mothers. But Colette makes us see what is possible when a fairly normal childhood, a certain amount of cultural permission for feminine creativity, and an absolute bedrock of mothering are present.

In her last thirty-five years Colette followed a sequence of religious deepening that many women have experienced but have never articulated or described. Because I hope that Colette's pattern is or can become that of most women, the last stages of her life are quite important in terms of the images and interests they reflect. I will emphasize her autobiographical works and memoir/ meditations, because in these works she confronted most directly the many forces of her life. She transcended down into the heart of All.

The figure of Sido, Colette's mother, began to emerge in her works when Colette was in her forties, and became more and more central to her experience as she moved toward old age and death. Sido's enjoyment of life never slackened; indeed, it became more passionate as she grew older and all life forms became more mysterious and intense to her. Sido gave her daughter the strength to hold out against patriarchal values and to individuate far beyond the social and personal perimeters that had sometimes stifled Sido's own development. Her mother's life seems to have been the central image of meditation and affirmation for Colette's passage into middle and old age; this image became Colette's metaphysical foundation, her image of the cosmos.

Colette tells us that the short pieces that make up *My Mother's House* (published in 1922) and *Sido* (1929) were composed off and on for several years before the works were put together. She was sixteen when her mother was fifty-five and thus remembered quite clearly her mother's passage from middle age to old age.

GATHERING THE MATRILINEAL THREADS: *MY MOTHER'S HOUSE*

It is remarkable how many male critics see Colette as purely sensuous and hence totally nonreligious.[1] Colette had early and deep connections to the cosmos and the natural world around her. Her mother participated in and yet royally dismissed the whole Catholic tradition; more important, as mother-priestess, Sido helped Colette through all the initiation rites that women undergo during life.

Colette was always skeptical of all claims of truth, an independent attitude learned early from her mother. For example, Sido established for Colette through her actions and everyday life a higher and different morality structure from any the church could possibly provide a female child. Sido cast strong doubt on ideas about immortality, the fulcrum of traditional religion:

> A ghost must be a wonderful thing to see. I only wish I could see one; I should call you at once if I did. Unfortunately, they don't exist. But if I could become a ghost after my death, I certainly should, to please you and myself too. And have you read that idiotic story about a dead woman's revenge? I ask you, did you ever hear such rubbish! What would be the use of dying if one didn't gain more sense by it? No, my child, the dead are a peaceful company. I don't fall out with my living neighbours, and I'll undertake to keep on good terms with the dead ones![2]

Riddled with inconsistencies, this statement nevertheless reveals an underlying respect for the idea of the moral development of the soul, and besides the wonderful energy of her mother's language, Colette carried away the idea of many possibilities for the soul.

Though adamantly anti-Catholic, Sido went to church. The priest of her village was of simple peasant stock and spent much of his time gardening. Upset at Colette's experience at catechism, Sido descended upon him, whereupon he gave her a cutting from a rare plant he had been jealously guarding. Sido responded to him as a human being with praiseworthy connections to earth and nature; ignoring his priesthood, she acceded to her inborn tact and returned home. Colette thus learned that people are more important than principles, that the natural goodness of individuals caught within the various malefic systems of patriarchy can release them from culpability. The old priest was kindly, not too bright, and clearly baffled by the energy and often brilliant willfulness of his free-thinking parishioner, yet he and Sido coexisted, essentially trusting one another. Such an attitude is more deeply reverent toward other humans than perhaps any of the church's tenets, which clearly never became part of Colette.

Sido's deepest influence on Colette came from her realm and being: she reigned in a prelapsarian *hortus conclusus*, an enclosed and sheltering garden, which represented a pre-Oedipal time of bliss and at-oneness with the mother and the natural world. The first two sections of *My Mother's House* evoke in Proustian detail this bipartite garden: "The Upper Garden overlooked the Lower Garden—a warm, confined enclosure . . . where the smell of tomato leaves mingled in July with that of the apricots ripening on the walls."[3] But the garden really existed only because of Sido's centrality to it; the garden was a mere extension of Sido's being. In the following splendid passage we see how Colette, sitting in the garden, needed the anchor of her mother to begin and end her days:

> In the house a lamp behind the sitting-room window suddenly glows red and the Little One [Colette] shivers. All that had looked green up to the moment before, now turns blue around this motionless red flame . . . It is the hour of lamps . . . The garden, grown suddenly hostile, menaces a now sobered little girl . . . The Little One, sitting on the grass, keeps her eyes fixed on the lamp, veiled for a moment by a brief eclipse. A hand has passed in front of the flame, a hand wearing a shining thimble. At the mere sight of this hand the Little One starts to her feet, pale, gentle now, trembling slightly as a child must who for the first

time ceases to be the happy little vampire that unconsciously drains the maternal heart; trembling slightly at the conscious realization that this hand and this flame, and the bent, anxious head beside the lamp, are the centre and the secret birthplace whence radiate in ripples ever less perceptible, in circles ever more and more remote from the essential light and its vibrations, the warm sitting room with its flora of cut branches and its fauna of peaceful creatures; the echoing house, dry, warm and crackling as a newly-baked loaf; the garden, the village. Beyond these all is danger, all is loneliness . . . the child's universe is bounded by the limits of a field, by the entrance of a shop, by the circle of light spreading beneath a lamp and crossed by a well-loved hand drawing a thread and wearing a silver thimble.[4]

The images of weaving, circles, the hearth flame, the mother's hands almost disembodied, fresh bread, the flora and fauna of this Peaceable Kingdom—this is cosmic unity and harmony without ritual liturgy. It simply is.

The strong and enduring priestess quality of Sido is further emphasized in allusions or descriptions of her body. Sido's gray eyes are described three times as severe and fearless;[5] the watchful ferocity of her protectiveness is thus presented. But her hands are mentioned at least fifteen times, and her arms several times too. Sometimes her hands are simply touching her children, but their visual effect is also emphasized: "Indignantly my mother folds her hands, pretty still though aging and weatherbeaten, over a bosom held up by gusseted stays."[6] Sido's arms carry her children with such care that she never lets their feet dangle or bang on things. Colette also remembers sleeping against her mother's knees, another image of the mother's statuary solidity, of the mother as *omphalos* (the navel of the universe).

Colette renders in especially powerful terms the transpersonal quality of the mother body in her narration of an event involving her oldest sister, Juliette. Juliette was forbidden by her new husband to speak to her parents because the Captain, Colette's father, had mismanaged and spent the dowry he owed his son-in-law's family. Colette watched her mother's responses as her alienated sister gave birth in the house next door:

Then a shadowy form in a white dressing gown—my mother—crossed the road and entered the garden opposite. I saw her raise her head and consider the party wall as though she had hopes of climbing it. Then she started to walk up and down the centre path . . . Under the cold light of the full moon not one of her gestures escaped me. Motionless, her face upturned to the sky, she listened, and waited. A thin cry, long-drawn-out and muffled by distance and the intervening walls, reached us at the same moment, and she clasped her hands convulsively to her breast. A second cry, pitched on the same note, almost like the opening of a melody, floated towards us, and a third. Then I saw my mother grip her own loins with desperate hands, spin around and stamp on the ground as she began to assist and share, by her low groans, by the rocking of her tormented body, by the clasping of her unwanted arms, and by her maternal anguish and strength, the anguish and strength of the ungrateful daughter who, so near to her, and yet so far away, was bringing a child into the world.[7]

This passage evokes the moon goddess, Artemis, who kills mothers by indifference—a cold goddess whom Sido placated by her spinning, rocking, circles of exorcism of her daughter's and her own pain. Colette also sees how peculiarly silent is this grief, the loss of a daughter, perhaps the deepest of feminine pain.

Sido felt for Juliette the same protectiveness that she did for Colette. She did not want Juliette to marry; she saw the new husband as a dangerous Pluto figure before he tipped his hand and demanded money. She did not really want either daughter to marry. In other, similar ways, Sido went against society; she never fired her pregnant servant girls and in fact told Colette, "After all, a lovely unrepentant creature, big with child, is not such an outrageous sight."[8] At a time when families threw out pregnant daughters or forced them to marry, Sido said she would never allow a man so irresponsible as to impregnate her daughter outside of marriage to take the girl from her hearth. Sido also hated funerals, refusing to give flowers for them; yet a visiting baby was encouraged to tear apart one of her most precious flowers, since she could see purpose to spending nature's bounty in that way.

Among Colette's initiations into adulthood was her recognition of shadow figures of herself and her mother, which enhanced the dimensions of the Demeter/Persephone possibilities. Colette juxtaposes with the tale of Juliette's giving birth a rather cool story of the village's most beautiful girl, who grew up thinking that a man would whirl her away into new and higher dimensions of reality. Sido admired the girl's beauty when she was a child, but remarked that the family of this girl, who grew up to be a seamstress, would hold her back. The girl did not finish school and could not find the perfect man; Colette sees her old and embittered, her beauty meaningless. The woman was finally lost to life because of her passive wait for what her beauty seemed to assure her: that someone else would confer meaning on her life. Sido told Colette about this pattern, but in this vignette we see that Colette had finally to internalize it. The girl was a shadow figure to Colette, who fell prey to the idea that her first husband would *be* her life pattern. By the time she told this tale, she was an independent older woman who knew that only she could transform her life, give it significance and pattern.

COLETTE IN HER FIFTIES:
HER ENTRANCE INTO OLD AGE
AND THE CRYSTALLIZATION OF THE GODDESS

When Colette wrote at about age fifty-six of her mother, Sido had become the godhead of maternity; the goddess of the four quarters, east, west, north, and south; the white witch of the winds. The garden had been subsumed to her being more surely at this time. Yet at the same time her shadow sides had gained more ferocity, more pull.

In *My Mother's House* Sido was the center of the house and garden, a goddess for the child in Colette, a Hestia figure. In *Sido*, a sequel, Sido became a goddess more befitting to the older Colette. The center of a larger universe, she stands at the center of the four winds, the cardinal points, knowing before anyone else what they were bringing. She looms tall in the center of her garden, honing her delicate responses as she turns in the wind. She stands at the center of the compass, reading the portents of winds, the moon, the zodiac. She forecasts the winter through studying onion skins or squirrel behavior. Our lady of the plants, Sido seems to make the plants grow. She ties them up with golden thread and visits them for a restorative, "lifting roses by the chin to look them full in the face."[9] She particularly loves red plants, especially in combination; the feminine affinity for the sacredness of blood is undoubtedly reflected here. Colette especially remembered a sudden spring snow which was first melted by the emerging red of the geranium, an image of the feminine red vanquishing the cold of whiteness. In her plant realm, Sido again preceded the church. When Colette brought home a blessed flower from the church, her mother laughed her irreverent laugh: "D'you suppose it wasn't already blessed before?"[10]

Colette never seemed to doubt the spiritual powers of her mother, even in the next world. Colette's strongest religious belief seems founded on the indomitable love her mother embodied. A most touching and beautiful image of perfect, disinterested, and receptive maternal love appears in *Sido*: her youngest son cried nightly for some particular food, but when Sido got it for him, he cried again. She pressed the child as to why, and he replied that he enjoyed crying for it. Many mothers might have been impatient, but Sido showed the best kind of reverential mothering; as the boy expressed his childish desire to cry for the ideal and unattainable, "Sido bent over him, as attentive as if he were an egg cracking as it began to hatch, or an unknown variety of rose, or a messenger from the other hemisphere."[11] Feminine endurance and patience, the waiting and watching as her child unfolded—this is what some less-than-perceptive men call passivity. But in the best tradition of mothering, Sido would not have dreamed of allowing her ego to intrude on a child's harmless fantasy. Instead, she tended to surround her children with love and care and let them grow as they would.

In *Sido* Colette seems aware of how her sense of self was crystallized at her mother's behest. As the following sequence shows, Sido gave Colette her initial experiences of autonomy and independence. In fact, Colette's original discovery of self came when her mother, as directing, knowing priestess, sent her off by herself before dawn to pick fruit. Because Colette so loved the dawn, she regarded this errand as a reward. She made a trip through the countryside that "described a great circle in the woods, like a dog out hunting on its own," and she tasted the water of "two hidden springs which I worshipped." One spring tasted of oak leaves, the other of iron and hyacinth stalks: "The more mention of them makes me hope that their savour may fill my mouth when my time comes, and that I may carry hence with me that imagined draught."[12] So she imagined her end as partaking of the delights of her beginning. In this ritual she first becomes truly self-aware: "It was on that road and at that hour that I first became aware of my own self, experienced an inexpressible state of grace, and felt one with the first breath of air that stirred, the first bird, and the sun so newly born that it still looked not quite round."[13]

Thus, before her first Mass, she experienced a pristine nature whose perfection gave her immortal yearnings and clues. She traced the perfect circle of her own being, visited the inner depths of herself, took communion with fresh fruit and spring water. Could the Eleusinian rites offer finer measures of and resources for feminine being? Sido and her daughter simply preceded church ritual, literally, metaphorically, and naturally.

Yet while Sido's goddess/priestess quality loomed larger, her shadow side became more attractive to Colette. Sido's strange friend Adrienne sharply embodied a feminine polarity to her:

> A lively creature, both alert and dreamy, with beautiful, yellow gipsy eyes beneath frizzy hair, she used to wander about in a sort of rustic rapture, as though daily impelled by some nomadic instinct. Her house resembled her in its untidiness and shared with her a grace denied to orderly places and people.[14]

As an eleven-year-old, Colette brooded over the story that Adrienne and Sido had exchanged babies once while nursing, blushing as she thought of "Adrienne's swarthy breast and its hard, purple knob." She began to visit and stay overlong at Adrienne's house, and the older women's friendship abruptly cooled. Sido apparently saw her daughter's unconscious erotic longing for the polar mother body: "It took me a very long time to associate a disturbing memory, a certain warmth in the heart, and the enchanted transformation of a person and her dwelling, with the idea of a first seduction."[15] This experience may have laid the ground for the consolation that Colette found in lesbian relationships between her first and second marriages. These women offered her the shelter of the mother body.

Colette also saw other dark sides of her mother, but it is important to realize that these aspects were not devouring or demonic, contrary to the male, Jungian precept that the dark and devouring side of the mother always coexists with the "good" side. Sido lived as an educated and fairly independent young woman among brothers who accepted her as a peer before her first and disastrous marriage. She was well read and occasionally took pleasure trips to Paris. She possessed "a sort of wild gaiety, a contempt for the whole world, a light-hearted disdain which cheerfully spurned [Colette] along with everything else."[16] These moments were "kindled by an urge to escape from everyone and everything, to soar to some high place where only her own writ ran," yet she always "returned to earth . . . weighed down with anxieties, and love, and a husband and children who clung to her."[17] This wild face of Sido is perhaps most apparent in a story she loved to tell, of the time when she was very pregnant and held a horse's head as a tornado dumped a whole harvest of frogs all over her. Once Sido admitted that she did not like visiting the sick: "and that sudden wild face of hers, free of all constraint, without charity or humanity, leapt out from behind her face of everyday."[18] Through example, Sido thus allowed Colette to have her own darker sides, and to acknowledge them. And I think she may have unconsciously delegated Colette to do the flying she so longed for and that her eldest daughter Juliette may have died from want of. (Remember Morrison's Pilate who flew though grounded.)

For all the weight that Sido bore as the center of the household, she was not protected from terrible casualties. She seemed to have attributed more symbolic than personal value to her husband, who went into jealous rages over her visits to the grocer even in his old age but was incapable of compassion when Sido had her breasts removed, four years apart. The older son, Achilles, became a doctor but died a saddened and bitter man. Colette's youngest brother never used his musical genius, around which Sido built great hopes, and revisited the family garden as an old man to grow furious that neighbors had changed, that new plants and even animals inhabited the lawns, and, most of all, that the gate had been oiled and lost its familiar sound. He seemed to search for the magic of Sido in the very place he grew up, whereas Colette in many ways became her mother.

Breast cancer is sometimes correlated with repressed anger. Did Sido's unrelenting role as Hestia cripple her, both intrapsychically and externally? Did the eldest daughter, Juliette, bear Sido's more severe ego projection and criticism, a usual fate for the eldest daughter? Did Colette, as the youngest daughter, receive some nurturing the others missed? Excessively dependent on her, did the males so polarize Sido, make her into a force different from themselves, that they negated her personality and hence never achieved a separate identity from her? This is perhaps the dark core at the heart of this autobiography, which the writer herself may not fully have recognized.

In Colette's consciousness, however, her mother was an almost wholly positive force. Colette internalized the *hortus conclusus* (enclosed garden) of her mother and could return and rest there within her own feminine self, which so emulated the best of Sido. Unlike her brothers, who regress to the enwombment of the mother house, Colette was able to internalize and become the goddess ground of being herself. She reinterpreted the goddess role within her own life and undoubtedly was stronger, better, for it.

THE GIFT OF SIDO'S LAST DAYS: COLETTE'S EMBRACE OF OLD AGE

Published one year before *Sido*, Colette's novel *Break of Day* portrays a woman who enters the last stage of life by saying goodbye to romantic relationships. The young lover is juxtaposed palely against the powerful image of Colette's mother in the very last years of her life, a time barely alluded to even in *Sido*. The novel is structured around excerpts from Sido's letters, each of which is a brick in the edifice of old age, the monument to serenity that Colette builds in this novel.

The novel opens by showing that Sido's maternal love, so central to her existence, finally lost power beside her love of the unfolding cosmos, as embodied by a pink cactus that flowered only every forty years. She chose to stay beside that cactus during her last year rather than visit Colette. Discussing her own aging, Colette reminded herself: "Let me not forget that I am the daughter of a woman who bent her head, trembling, between the blades of a cactus, her wrinkled face full of ecstasy over the promise of a flower, a woman who herself never ceased to flower, untiringly during three quarters of a century."[19]

Letter by letter, the novel reveals attributes of strength and love of life, which should be read several times by any woman on the threshold of old age. Two final examples show how Sido faced death. First, Sido relates the visit of her granddaughter to her final sickbed: "Eight years old, her black locks all tangled, for she had run to bring me a rose. She remained on the threshold of my room, as alarmed by my waking as by my sleep. I shall see nothing before my death as beautiful as that shy child, who wanted to cry and held out a rose."[20] This is an evocation of the Persephone of the Future, even in the last days of life.

Second, Sido's last written words became a hieroglyph of hope to Colette:

> No doubt my mother wrote that last letter to assure me that she no longer felt any obligation to use our language. Two pencilled sheets have on them nothing more than apparently joyful signs, arrows emerging from an embryo world, little rays, "yes, yes" together, and a single "she danced," very clear. Lower down she had written "my treasure"—her name for me when our separations had lasted a long time and she was longing to see me again. But this time I feel a scruple in claiming for myself so burning a word. It has a place among strokes, swallow-like interweavings, plant-like convolutions—all messages from a hand that was trying to transmit to me a new alphabet or the sketch of some ground-plan envisaged at dawn under rays that would never attain the sad zenith. So that instead of confused delirium, I see in that letter one of those haunted landscapes where, to puzzle you, a face lies hidden among the leaves, an arm in the fork of a tree, a body under a cluster of rock.[21]

The organic, birdlike quality of the alphabet Sido senses at the edge of the spirit world, the lines radiating from the sunlike "yes, yes," her final salute to her treasured daughter—these signs all suggest the joyful transition that Sido found in death.

Break of Day ends with a gentle, dewy, cold, blue dawn that symbolizes a certain mourning over the loss of youth yet promises a new spirituality, a higher life state, a different kind of beginning. The novel's imagery suggests that Sido became enwombed in Colette's heart as she died to the world: "I felt stirring at the root of my being the one who now inhabits me, lighter on my heart than I was once in her womb."[22] With *Sido* and *Break of Day* Colette consolidated and established the fortress of her feminine origins.

Colette's last two memoirs, *The Evening Star* and *The Blue Lantern*, on the other hand, are the liveliest portraits of a woman in the last stages of life that presently exist. These two books have been neglected, at least partly because they are not easy going for younger readers. Their structure is meditative, reflective, though unified through imagery and certain literary techniques. Another stumbling block, perhaps, is that to enjoy them one must depend somewhat on a knowledge of Colette's life and other works. In these books she delineates for us the memories that became forces of survival for her, and we can learn some saving attitudes toward even such endings to life as invalidism.

The Evening Star, a reference to Venus, published in 1946 when Colette was seventy-three, was the first book she ever wrote without a deadline and without desire for or assurance of publication. She addresses us as "hypothetical readers" and speaks several times of the pleasure of writing only what she really thinks and feels rather than dressing it up as fiction. Like Pilate in *Song of Solomon*, she has arrived at a point where neither fear nor ambition hampers her direct perception of life.

This book is more akin to memoirs than to autobiography, though the modes mingle and unify into a really unique literary work. Colette reminds us frequently that she writes from a new perspective, that of a bedridden invalid taking a contemplative position in life. This perspective becomes almost a persona by the end of the book, which is punctuated with dialogue between herself and her husband, Maurice Goudeket, followed by what she is really thinking and feeling. In other words, she takes the reader into the heart of the persona, reminding us that no one, even someone trapped in a bed and apparently totally vulnerable, is only what you see or hear.

Colette's illness is important in establishing the character of her narrator. Her lifelong servant, Pauline, and Maurice Goudeket apparently loved taking care of Colette, who took on the positive role of the invalid, making others feel needed, useful, important, strong. Her strength of character even at this time of complete physical dependence shows also in her attitude toward sedatives and pain-killers, which she refused even to unseal though they lay on her bed table; she enjoyed her clarity of thought too much to take them. She even regarded her pain as something against which she could affirm her integrity:

> I hesitate to call those nights bad that the arthritis chooses to torment my leg and hip. There is, in the pain that comes in bursts or waves, an element of rhythm which I cannot entirely condemn, a flux and reflux whose autonomy grips the attention. What I call honourable suffering is my dialogue with the presence of this evil. [23]

This same lucidity helped Colette to perceive and write of the new quality of time she found in being an old person. She muses:

> The day turns towards evening. Is not everything evening, vespers, for me? The days not so much miserly as rapid. Is not the sixth boy who was born this week under my window [the apartment beneath hers] beginning to walk? The oldest of the six, shepherd of this male flock, leads it to the garden, where it scatters . . . They grow like chickens . . . and I get mixed up among them. Everything alters the moment I take my eyes off it. The life of a virtually immobilized being is a vortex of hurry and variety.[24]

Besides the clearness of her vision, Colette reveals other sides of her character. Important to her feminine metaphysics, and an attitude undoubtedly learned from Sido, is her simple and passionate love for what simply is — her excited and devoted study of each event or person for all its complexity and its contradictory sides. We see, for example, the depth of vision she has attained through her unflinching, even fascinated, view of the human underworld. She argues implicitly against modesty or moral censorship in women's journey through the world, discussing her experience with transvestites, exhibitionists, black marketeers, and a homosexual editor with a hilarious taste for young and handsome policemen. She had an intermittent relationship with a man who occasionally made an obscene phone call to her:

> It is two or four o'clock in the morning . . . He asks if it is I, really I, and I assure him it is. Then he says: "I shit on you," and hangs up again — too soon, for I should like to question him about his mysterious ailment, for the motives of his insomnia, to discover whether, having nocturnally shit on me, he can fall back on his bed to sleep there, at last happy and released. As it happens, he is discreet, only wakes me at long intervals, and utters only that, shall I say, essential word.[25]

Never does she condemn any of these various twists and turns of the human psyche. She seems always to have understood the complications of sexuality and how its compulsions make the imposition of moral values difficult, at best.

The fully individuated matriarch does not, however, passively acquiesce to all that she has examined and experienced. Colette does acknowledge the existence of evil. Throughout the book she attempts over and over to absorb and assimilate the meaning of the

Nazi occupation of Paris. The bitterest passages — perhaps the only bitter ones — in all of her work concern the Nazi treatment of the Jews:

> There were also — profound terror, agitation of our hearts — the cries and appeals of a night when the enemy took away the Jewish children of the district and their mothers, separated the Jewish husbands from their wives, and caged the men in one van, the women and children, sorted out, in two other vans . . . Can I compare my own nightmare of absence to such separations as these? I do not dare, since my own came to an end . . .[26]

Her husband was among those taken away by the Nazis. Colette did all she could to get him released, but her moral integrity stopped her from the one act that would have placed her with those who turned their eyes from the plight of the French Jews during the Occupation:

> A collaborator explained to her that he had got from the Germans permanent employment for Maurice in the camp, and special treatment, if in return Maurice would inform on his companions. "I refuse," said Colette calmly. "I don't think you quite understand. The alternative is death. Death, do you understand, death." "Very well then, I choose death." "Not without consulting your husband, I imagine!" "*We* choose death," amended Colette.[27]

So much has been written on the male experience of war; war probably is a masculine archetype (that is, an image all or mainly carried in the collective unconscious of men) too often brought to terrible and literal fruition. Colette gives us instead the woman's point of view: the terrible waiting; the courage of local prostitutes, embroideresses, and others who confronted the enemy through their own oblique ways of resistance. The waiting women only gradually realized that systematic genocide evolved from the first arrests; as usual, they were left out of the action, yet had to digest the ultimate meaning to be found in the deranged idiocy of such inhumanity. Was not the Nazi phenomenon the most pathological phase of masculine analysis and its scientific, "objectifying" technology?

An important aspect of matriarchal wisdom might be an aversion to the bodies of theory behind which patriarchal pathology hides its often murderous intent. Colette tells us that she always had an aversion to politics and that as an old woman, she distrusts general principles. She gently parodies the young interviewers who come to her bedside, sure that she is hiding some philosophy from them:

> What can be more normal than to quake in the presence of the young? . . . They think that I have some general ideas. It is not for me to inform them that I exist on those funds of frivolity that come to the aid of the long-lived. That a time comes when one has to choose between bitterness, pessimism as it used to be called, and its opposite, and that my choice was made long since — or let us say, more accurately, that it is flaunted. [28]

She thus boils down her general principle to an attitude, and she perhaps names at least the genesis of that attitude: "What don't I owe to my credulity? As they say in my natal province, 'If I believe, the evil is not great, afterwards I can stop believing.'" [29] This of course reflects a certain French stoicism, such as Pascal's, in the face of an ambiguous universe. But Colette goes further and approaches everything believing in its own originality. Such matriarchal, situational ethics do not let a person flounder with no beliefs because of the relativity of all things, but rather give an individual the ability to believe in everything at once until absolute proof of inauthenticity presents itself.

Colette found such meaning in relationships, especially those she had with women, rather than in general principles. Like most women, she meditates upon the lives of her friends and sees that there are differences between these lives. She spends about twelve pages telling us the story of Helen Picard, a beautiful tribute to extrafamilial feminine bonds. She mentions Maurice's chagrin at Helene's treatment of him as one of Colette's passing fancies — an amusing aside that reflects the tendency of women with longstanding friendships to see their friends' mates as transient, compared to them. Women know that they will continue their bonds with their friends to the grave, while lovers and spouses are too often serial in nature. Colette remembers so many wonderful details of Helene, such as her wrapping cake or cheese in recently written poems, airily remarking she can write more, or her approbation of male homosexuality yet horror at the idea of women making love. Colette rather disagrees with such opinions, but as they are part of her friend she accepts and loves them, even Helene's tendency toward self-destruction.

Although Colette's last books scarcely mention Sido, one senses her presence in the deep and strong connections Colette has with other women; these bonds seem to ground and connect Colette to her time of history in a way that perhaps the grandmother/mother/granddaughter linkage cannot. A woman's strong bonds with her own age group (such as Colette's female literary friends) may anchor her in her own generation. Colette thus had roots in time that were both broad and deep, matriarchal and matrilineal.

In this vein, Colette recounts an interesting episode. Through strange and fortuitous twistings of fate, she found and bought a picture of Sido's mother, who died young, leaving Sido to the care of an arbitrary and unloving father. Colette was happy to have the picture of this grandmother: "She smiles, well content — to my mind — to have regained the corner of my mantelpiece . . . all I know about her is her premature death and her silence as a betrayed wife . . . I love to see her at peace in my home."[30] It is as if Colette knew she was exposing the anonymity and suffering of our foremothers to clarity and light; as she says in Sido, "To me the important thing is to lay bare and bring to light something no human eye before mine has gazed upon."[31] I think the feminine cosmos gave Colette her grandmother's portrait as an emblem of how she recovered and gave wholeness and light to the silence and fragmentation of many women's lives.

Colette shows how women have always been survivors, remaining as the earth does after the cataclysms that men have too often caused:

> To live, to survive . . . After so many years of war these words possess immense importance. The will to survive is so alive in us women, and the lust for physical victory is so female! When they notice it, our men can't get over seeing us so ferocious . . . it is very probable that ferocity is our accustomed climate. Nevertheless, I am shocked by masculine moderation . . .[32]

She was writing here of Maurice's ability to forgive and forget what the Nazis did to him. Yet even her own bitterness gave way to a mellower vision, and this final affirmation of life has a greater depth, I believe, because of the evil that she lived through.

In a way, *The Evening Star* is a stripping away of the chaff of life, those things that do not or should not matter. Colette could not quite reject the experience of evil she suffered under the Nazis; it appears to have been etched into her nervous system. But she did divest herself of the need for a loving audience in her writing. She cleaned out her drawers and threw away all that she did not want discovered at her death in the course of writing this book. She also tossed away the criticism she had from male reviewers who (understandably) did not like her portrait of Cheri and some of the other males in her novels. She says she obtained her critics' reward from women alone and mentions women who approached her after seeing the play of Cheri, saying only, "Ah yes, yes!" or "Ah, the swine . . . ," with such fervor that she needed no more reassurance that she had struck a nerve, rendered a truth. She also became bemused by medical cures, remarking on them all as fashions that a young male doctor takes on as part of his persona. She tried on cures much as she tried on the many careers of her life, shucking each off as she tried it.

What remains is central: Maurice and Pauline, who mother her into the arms of death, and her memories. She saves the best for last; in the twelfth chapter she recounts the birth of her only child, her daughter, Bel-Gazou, who was born when Colette was forty. In this way she finally, at age seventy-three, wrote of an experience that symbolized the whole mystery and joy of creation, an experience she clearly turned over and over, internalizing its mystical quality, showing how central it was to her attitude of on-goingness and joy in living. Colette captures the mystery we take for granted:

> The outcome is the contemplation of a new person who has entered the house without coming in from outside . . . her nails, resembling in their transparency, the convex scale of the pink shrimp—the soles of her feet, which have reached us without touching the ground . . . the light plummage of her lashes, lowered over her cheek, interposed between the scenes of earth and bluish dream of her eye . . .[33]

Both by the way she wrote and by the arrangement of topics in *The Evening Star*, Colette shows us that giving birth was a central metaphysical and mystical experience that increasingly became a source of cosmic affirmation for her. How many old women likewise turn over the lessons of their younger bodies but are afraid to speak of them, fearing that the projections of "sterile old bag," "witch," "dried-up crone" that others carry will make them bear the labels of "unseemly" and "indecorous" as well? Women have been so deeply engrained with the idea that their biological functions are shameful that too many repress this kind of memory and knowledge.

Finally, let us take a brief look at the images of death with which Colette ends the book. Throughout *The Evening Star* she sorts memories and photographs, saving the ones that are most precious for those who will remain after her. She is quite conscious of the fact that death could take her soon; she remarks on the worn underside of her right sleeve, saying that a new blouse need not be very long-wearing. She further notes that at her age her mother was still wrestling huge chests around the house, but that she, Colette, is able only to work tapestry. After discussing the beautiful colors and textures, the sensuousness that she finds in embroidery, she speculates that she will probably also continue writing, despite the physical difficulty of doing so. She ends with this masterful, imaginative paragraph:

> On a resonant road the trotting of two horses harnessed as a pair harmonizes, then falls out of rhythm to harmonize anew. Guided by the same hand, pen and needle, the habit of work and the common sense desire to bring it to an end become friends, separate, come together again . . . Try to travel as a team, slow chargers of mind; from here I can see the end of the road.[34]

There is a certain tender ferocity in Colette's sense that she could let go of other long-term goals but not of the art of writing, though she would have to intersperse it with the less trying daily task of pondering over her needlework. This is an image not of death, but of an open road. She must have sensed that she had more work to do, a longer life ahead of her, another book to bequeath us.

Much more of a journal than *The Evening Star*, *The Blue Lantern* (1949) steeps one in the day-to-day concerns of the aged and increasingly ill Colette. The work is elegaic, full of "last things."

Colette begins by explaining that since her eyesight and hearing are failing a bit, her world is more and more contained within the blue light on her bedside table. The color blue was always special to her. In *The Break of Day*, it was sometimes fearful, a cold beginning to an end: "The cold blue has crept into my bedroom, trailing after it a very faint tinge of flesh colour that clouds it. It is the dawn, wrested from the night, drenched and chill."[35] But blue is also the deep, unending space of mystery: "The unfathomable blue of the night, powdered with stars, makes my rather bare pink walls look pinker still when I turn and look at them."[36] Or it is spiritual: "Everything is less blue today. Or else it may be me. Blueness is mental. Blue doesn't make you hungry, or voluptuous. A blue room is uninhabitable . . . Unless you no longer hope for anything—in which case you can live in a blue room."[37]

In *The Blue Lantern* Colette further says, "There must be some reason why we find ourselves so sensibly affected by blue: Age-old evocations of the firmament, a moist mirage in desert eyes, all that we hold to be eternal, is readily blue."[38] Of the blue lantern itself, she wrote at length:

> I ride at anchor beneath the blue lantern, which is quite simply a powerful commercial lamp at the end of a lengthy extensible arm, fitted with a blue bulb and a blue paper shade. Though a permanent fixture, it has none the less suggested to my neighbours the name they have chosen to baptise it with —*fanal*—the light that rakes the seas.[39]

Thus Colette's bed becomes a self-enclosed system that obliterates the distinctions around it, such as night and day. It is a ship that casts off its moorings from the physical limitations of the world; imagination and a sense of adventure become the rudder. Sea imagery is important:

> Instead, then, of landing on new islands of discovery, is my course set for the open sea where there is no sound other than that of the lonely heart-beat comparable to the pounding of the surf? Rest assured, nothing is decaying, it is I who am drifting . . . The open sea, but not the wilderness. The discovery that there is no wilderness! That in itself is enough to sustain me in triumphing over my afflictions.[40]

Remember in *My Mother's House* Colette's sense of self as a young sailor, her mother's sewing hands a sort of beacon at the window. In *The Blue Lantern* she continues this image of life: the cosmos closes in with its mists of mystery as her blue and contemplative light bobs in the nighttime of her life, lit by the unquenchable fire within her. This image, I believe, rests on Colette's early sense of the cosmos as a benign and receptive mother, a symbolic reading of the universe which she gained from her mother, Sido.

The other affirmative image occurs at the very end of the book. Colette has been offered many pets, but refuses, saying:

The only living animal left to me that I can call my own is the fire. It is my guest, and the work of my hands. I know all about covering a fire, succouring a fire. I know the art of surrounding a fire in the open air with a circular trench, so that it may burn up well without "marking" the stubble and setting the ricks ablaze. I am well aware of its dislike of even numbers, that three logs burn better than two and seven than four, and that like every other animal, it likes having its belly scratched from underneath . . . I give it its quota of splinters, twigs and dried leaves, and I intend always to have the last word with it — that stand-by of trainers acquired through long dealings with animals. It repays me, by hurling itself upon the least of my offerings; it makes much of me, encourages me in my by now automatic incantations to it: the business of incantation loses nothing by it.

The hearth at which I solemnize my fire worship is of ancient construction . . .[41]

The fire of life, the Hestian principle of process, the turning of raw material to energy — Colette here symbolizes her life force as a trustworthy animal who burns bright, sharing the light that is cast by the blue lantern. She has become a Vestal Virgin, keeping the fire in a circle, tending it, she says, "ceaselessly."

Within this fire of self, Colette accepted, more truly than in *The Evening Star*, the insurrection of the spirit that made writing her destiny to the end; she could not stop. At the end of *The Blue Lantern* she wrote, "You may read the words 'To be continued . . . ,'[42] and with these words she concluded this last book. Throughout her life, she vividly portrayed the woman who can survive anything, and became that woman.

It is important finally to examine Colette's own death as an image bequeathed to us just as she left us Sido's death. In his *Close to Colette*, her last husband, Maurice Goudeket, writes of her spiritual awareness of the universe:

Before every manifestation of life, animal or vegetable, she felt a respect which resembled religious fervor. At the same time she was always aware of the unity of creation in the infinite diversity of its forms.

One evening she gave me a striking example of this. We were at the cinema, watching one of those shorts which show germination accomplished in a moment, unfolding of petals which look like a struggle, a dramatic dehiscence. Colette was beside herself. Gripping my arm, her voice hoarse and her lips trembling, she kept on saying with the intensity of a pythoness, "There is only one creature! D'you hear, Maurice, there is only *one* creature."[43]

This philosophy is imaged again in her last words and action before dying:

Two days before the end, she emerged from a great weariness into an hour of great lucidity . . . It was a hot August day with a veiled sky. The swallows were passing level with the open window, with sharp whirrings. Colette bent toward me and I put my head against her side. She pointed to the boxes of butterflies on their shelf, the book, and the birds in the garden. "Ah!" she said. So near to death and knowing it, everything appeared to her more beautiful and more wonderful than ever. Her hands fluttered about her like wings. She leaned a bit closer to me. Her arm described a spiral which embraced everything that she had shown me: "Look!" she said to me. "Maurice, look!"[44]

From these passages as well as the whole span of her work we see that Colette's philosophy contained no dualism of spirit and body, divinity and nature; she sees unity in the cosmos, not in hierarchy. She transcends down, becomes a deep diver into the murky telepathic connections that flow between seemingly separate human psyches. She transcends down into the nonrational and chthonic sphere. No wonder that her religious awareness, her metaphysics, could not be bound by words, by dogmas, or by religious institutions. She was too attentive and reverent to all manifestations of reality.

III
KNOWLEDGE FROM
THE BODIES OF WOMEN

The three chapters in this section consider knowledge gleaned from the matriarchal body in terms of symbols, spiritual knowledge, and morality. Chapter IX concentrates on alchemical, mythic, and organic symbols, including some new symbols that might be helpful to modern women's self-definition. Jung viewed alchemical writings as a stream of underground, repressed thought that for centuries ran counter to the official Judeo-Christian traditions. He studied it as symbolic of psychic wholeness, of the creative and collective unconscious, and of ego consciousness. Chapter X explores how various occult traditions better reflect women's pluralistic, matrilineal, earthy sense of the sacral than most of the Judeo-Christian traditions; the quality of women's faith is also explored. A feminine cosmology and ethos will be suggested for the reader's consideration. Chapter XI considers problems and questions that are the crux of feminine moral dilemmas; women's ethics and morality of agape, responsibility, and caretaking are defined.

9. Symbols of the Feminine

The alchemical images for gender differences can be especially illuminating if augmented or reinterpreted from a feminine perspective. The alchemists' attempt to render reality in terms of minerals gives us some wonderfully rich, connotative gender essences.

For example, they usually regarded the masculine principle as a combination of fire, air, and sulfur; the feminine principle as water, earth, and salt.[1] The male elements are active, caustic, dangerous, consuming (reflecting Oedipal separation and hunger), while the female are passive, flowing, nurturing, containing, solid, reassuring, preserving. These lists could be divisive if alchemists did not insist that each group must connect with the other for completion to form a mystical union. The element that combines the two principles is mercury, which unites the sulfur and the salt; each individual must work toward this connection, which seems to come in middle age, perhaps as mature wisdom. It is as if each person must arrive at the specific wisdom of her or his own gender before she or he can touch and connect with the wisdom of the other sex.

Remember that the god Mercury, or Hermes, is the god with wings at his heels. He has no home on Olympus, but rather flits about from god to goddess or from the underworld to the sea; he is always on the move, on the road, connecting diverse realms. Mercury is an emblem of the imagination, which can contain and connect the whole cosmos. And only through imagination can a person understand the opposite sex's experience of the body, parenting, and incarnation itself.

I will leave it to someone else to determine whether the paradigm of fire, air, and sulfur is a fruitful image for men. I have certainly found water, earth, and salt to be metaphors that deepen and enrich theories of the feminine psyche. The ancient keeper of the hearth, for example, the goddess Hestia, is a virgin mother in whom salt and earth commingle to provide the family container, the home and hearth; she is the salt—the feminine wisdom, the sweat of the process, the labor—that supports the home. But in all Hestia cults, water—the fertilizing element, the image of softening, playful fecundity—is forbidden. Water is Venus's element; it implies change and development. Water dissolves, changes, flows, and carries our affections to many destinations that bring richness and growth. When a woman enacts the archetype of Hestia, she is virgin, that is, an unchanging, faceless love and perimeter. If she lives out only that role, she is perhaps doomed to changelessness; she never journeys but is the destination for the journeyer.

However, we need to enlarge the feminine principle's triad. Penelope Shuttle and Peter Redgrove in *The Wise Wound* brilliantly expound at length on the omnipresence of the element of blood in all ritual. [2] Yet fear of menstrual and birth blood is almost universal in the masculine psyche. I think the element of blood is central to (and perhaps is the sum of) the feminine. Earth, water, and salt may implicitly commingle in blood, which is the messenger of birth or of the monthly death of potential new life in the womb. Woman's blood can become a literal baby. One of Sylvia Plath's most memorable lines is to her infant son in "Nicholas and the Candlestick": "The blood blooms clean/ In you, ruby." [3] And it may be that women must insist upon blood as a nontaboo part of their being and presence. I believe that the harmless and reassuring cycle of the blood from their own bodies and their experiences of the waxing and waning of their energies as they synchronize with this cycle at least partially underlie women's sense of death as part of an ongoing cycle, not to be feared.

The masculine psyche seems usually to render death as a kind of solar extinguishment. Apollo, the archer/son, strikes and destroys from afar, but Diana/moon only eclipses. The east/west orientation of the Hestia/Vesta cult teaches us how woman's body is the symbol of the beginning and the ending; woman's body also gives her the sense of unity that most centers and focuses the feminine psyche in its transformative vision. The menstrual cycle is one of life and death; its very regularity teaches woman of the power and beneficence of nature and her body. Menopause releases the psyche from this, but her cycle is still a grounding knowledge of many years.

Jung has rather enigmatically written that the masculine principle is perfection; the feminine principle, completion. The number three is incomplete; the number four is the mandala, completion. Blood completes the feminine triad of earth, salt, and water and perhaps is that from which feminine wisdom flows, the true essence of woman, the Holy Grail that brims with blood, the fount of life.

The last section of Ellen Bass's poem "Tampons" is a visionary celebration of the emergence of this element. The blood power and essence of woman surface in an apocalypse of birth and renewal as the poet rejects all the devices for stopping up menstrual blood:

Okay. It's like the whole birth control schmear.
There just isn't a good way. Women bleed.
We bleed.
The blood flows out of us. So we will bleed.
Blood paintings on our thighs, patterns
like river beds, blood on the chairs in
insurance offices, blood on Greyhound buses
and 747's, blood blots, flower forms
on the blue skirts of the stewardesses.
Blood on restaurant floors, supermarket aisles, the steps of
     government
buildings. Sidewalks
                                             Gretel's bread
                 will have
                            blood trails,
crumbs. we can always find our way.
We will start to recognize each other by smell.
We will ease into rhythm together, it happens
when women live closely — African tribes, college sororities —
our blood flowing on the same days. The first day
of our heaviest flow we will gather in Palmer, Massachusetts,
on the steps of Tampax, Inc. We'll have a bleed in.
We'll smear the blood on our faces. Max Factor
will join OB in bankruptcy. The perfume
industry will collapse, who needs
whale sperm, turtle oil, when we have free blood?
For a little while cleaning products will boom,
409, Lysol, Windex. But
the executives will give up. The cleaning woman is leaving

a red wet rivulet, as she scrubs down the previous stains.
It's no use. The men would have to
do it themselves, and that will never come up
for a vote at the Board. Women's clothing manufacturers, fancy
furniture, plush carpet, all will phase out. It's just not
practical. We will live the old ways.
Simple floors, dirt or concrete, can be hosed down,
or straw can be cycled through the compost.
Simple clothes, none in summer. No more swimming pools.
Swim in the river. Yes, swim in the river. Everyone
come and swim in the river. Dogs will fall in love
with us. We'll feed the fish with our blood. Our blood
will neutralize the chemicals and dissolve the old car parts.
Our blood will detoxify the phosphates and the
PCB's. Our blood will feed the depleted soils.
Our blood will water the dry, tired surface of the earth.
We will bleed. We will bleed. We will
bleed until we bathe her in our blood and she turns
slippery like a baby birthing.[4]

In this poem blood becomes the bonding element that washes the
world clean and holds it together in a saving grace reminiscent of
Anne Sexton's image of women's milk as cosmic grace. We should
remember that breast milk and blood are but two sides of the
elemental feminine. Milk is perhaps refined blood. The loss of
blood can become a metaphor for feminine individuation, as in
Grace Paley's poignant "Living," in which the protagonist, Faith, is
bleeding uncontrollably after an abortion; her friend Ellen also
bleeds, eventually to death. Faith's loss of her friend and of
feminine blood are for her the same. Even in the first act of love a
very few young women bleed in such an unstinting way that some
have actually bled to death, like the character Esther almost does in
Sylvia Plath's *The Bell Jar*. The depth of woman's genitals can bring
the dark centeredness of feminine sexual pain; perhaps the female
ability to bleed suggests how far into the center of body/self/ego
woman's gender consciousness roots itself. Consider, then, how
differently men and women may view blood issuing from their
bodies.

If four is the number of completion, five is a holy number, the
Virgin Mary's number, the number of petals on a basic flower form.

So a fifth element that I want to claim as an image of the feminine par excellence is glass. Glass represents the refined, modern feminine psyche, a prism or perspective which will reveal anew all reality. We have new female typologies in modern women's fiction; we need a contemporary substance to symbolize the refining of the feminine psyche as it is burnished and polished by passing its days working in the fire of the patriarchy. Women have been depicted *with* glass—looking in mirrors, acting as mirrors to men, standing at windows longing for the return of soldiers, lovers. My images of glass are more internal, representing women's permeable ego boundaries. Glass contains; you can see into it, yet it shuts off, guards, is a protective shield although it lets light through in both directions.

My own best dreams of transformation have been of stained-glass structures (buildings, churches, arenas, flowers) that were organic yet at the same time emitted and captured light: spirituality as nature, manifesting through an art form that is vegetative. Stained glass, of course, captures the purity of white light split into the spectrum for manifestation in the natural world.

Women artists seem often fascinated with glass. Anaïs Nin spent hours as a child peering through different panes of a window in her home; she gave glass objects to people who, she thought, especially needed to see *through* to an essential and deeper reality beyond ego consciousness. Colette collected glass paperweights; here are some objects she searched for as she traveled through France:

> I couldn't tear myself away from a little shop under the arcades which sold—not to be found, even then—magnificent marbles, 'taws' stuffed with varicoloured spirals, as beautiful as the 'sulphurs' . . . In Avignon I rushed through my autograph session, after my 'chat,' to hurry to Señor Rafael Paz y Ferrer in his house of marvels, brimming with mother of pearl, twisted glassware, rainbow-dripping chandeliers, pearled embroidery.[5]

In literature by women, windows frequently frame a Penelope-like woman who stands for the journeyer's homecoming; windows, after all, connect home to community, turn the family outward, and women often mediate at that juncture. Women's perspective then becomes a new window, a view upon all that has only been seen patriarchally before. Glass also reminds us of the astral white light that meditators claim surrounds and protects them as they enter a trance. If women in the business world or in academia, where they feel their values threatened or at least in a minority, can imagine themselves as surrounded by a soft, glasslike boundary, they might find themselves more comfortable, more steady. They will be protected but also able to shed their special light and influence.

Glass, of course, is a new symbol for imagining the feminine principle. Older symbols are meaningful too, but women need to examine them carefully for their contemporary relevance. The moon and Venus are both important symbols of the feminine in astrology. Astrologers generally treat the moon as representative of an unconscious emotional substratum, while Venus is more specifically symbolic of the feminine. In 1941 Marc Edmund Jones defined Venus in the traditional way as a "circle of spirit placed on top of the cross of matter" which symbolizes "simple pleasure and appreciation in life."[6] In another book of the same year he went more deeply and subjectively into the meaning of Venus, projecting negativity and lowliness on her; Venus has an

acquisitive capacity . . . in a very literal or objective sense . . . [It stands for] ordinary routine activity in the conservation and refinement of things . . . and in the consumption, condemnation and destruction of them . . . [It is] the negative planet in the department, identifying the ulterior and aesthetic application of an individual's energies to the immediate problems of the group economy . . . [while Mars is] outreach, initiative, exterior . . . the positive planet.[7]

Jones is generally clearer than this, and the obfuscation suggests his rather sputtering resentment toward Venus. It is not clear why Venus is "the negative planet in the department," although Jones admires Mars for its more expansive nature. Perhaps he sees the Devouring Mother in Venus's "consuming" actions. His preference for Mars could also reflect what Jung called the pathological tendency towards total extroversion in American culture.[8] Another traditionalist, Stephen Arroyo, agrees with this interpretation and adds that Venus represents "the capacity for conscious relationship with another human being."[9]

Like Jones, Dane Rudhyar, the father of modern astrologers, tended to understand Venus by juxtaposing her with Mars, but he also brought to light her biological and positive attributes:

Martian impulse returns home filled with experiences. Venus is the end of the experience and what we have gathered as a result of it; thus it is the purveyor of consciousness, of knowledge and wisdom to the ego. It is symbolized by bees, because bees bring back to the hive the honey gathered from the flowers which are also the last product of the plant. It is therefore the symbol of all arts, of all social wisdom, of all that is matured out of experience. It also means emotions; because we get emotions, or effects, as a result of our outer contacts. Out of relationships arise joy or pain, songs or despair, art or sensuality. The soul of relations is love. Mars-love is the love that is desire, self-projection, brute force toward self-reproduction in and through others, but with no regard for others. Venus-love is the love that is wise, the love that arises from true interchange, from altruistic companionship: love, wisdom . . . Venus is self-reproduction . . . demonstrated in the power to bear children or ideas.[10]

For Rudhyar, Venus seems to represent the introspection that follows experience and bears wisdom, love from contact with and understanding of others. This is the honey we bring home from excursions into the outside world. Nevertheless, Rudhyar (writing in 1936) still saw Venus mainly as a response to Mars. These descriptions insist on woman defining herself in relationship to the masculine principle. There is no sense of woman alone, complete in herself before or outside of relationship.

A woman astrologist, Liz Greene, echoed this synthesis in a much more recent work (1978):

Venus symbolizes the need to share with another, even to the point of being subsumed; Mars [is] the passion which seeks to expend itself on another, and to reach an objective goal. Mars desires; Venus is the urge to be desired. Venus allows us to recognize that we are in relationship with others and, by comparisons, seeks to discover the similarities; Mars enables us to impose our way despite others, and through self-assertion, exposes the differences.[11]

Venus . . . is personal taste, what one seeks in a relationship . . . Venus and the moon are more accessible energy for women.[12]

Greene's Venus seeks to discover psychological similarities with others and is in danger of being subsumed therein. This sounds much like what some modern women sociologists are trying to say is basic to the psychology of women. Ann Bedford Ulanov, a theologian, defines matriarchal wisdom as "both/and" reasoning versus patriarchal reasoning of "either/or" which concurs with Greene's interpretation.[13] Similarly, Carol Gilligan, in her writings on women's morality, asserts that women live and think contextually, that their morality shifts according to the different needs of the people with whom they deal, that women's ethics are much more attuned to the situation than men's are.[14]

My favorite astrologist is Alice A. Bailey, though her work is very unclear. Her 1951 definition of Venus can be read as a vision of the impact the feminist movement has had on mass consciousness. Her description of Venus's powers does not depend on a contrast to the masculine principle in any way. Bailey does not even mention Mars:

> In the Aquarian Age the power of . . . Venus becomes dominant . . .
> Venus was the planet which we are told was responsible for the appear-
> ance of the individualized consciousness in man . . . In the Aquarian
> Age, Venus will again have an analogous influence only with this differ-
> ence that the emergence into manifestation of an increased individual-
> ism and self-conscious realisation will be subordinate to the appearance
> of the first stages of an expanded consciousness throughout all man-
> kind—the consciousness of group responsibility.[15]

She has earlier told us that in their developing the spiritual side of Venus, initiates learn that

> the Son of God who is The Son of Mind is the instrument of God's love;
> he must learn therefore, to transmute knowledge into wisdom.[16]

The highest attribute of God, his wisdom, is symbolized by Venus. In other words Bailey sees Venus, the feminine principle, as becoming stronger in our time; she teaches that individualism must become integrated into group responsibility and that knowledge without the wisdom to use it is antithetical to love. And it is through Venus that wisdom comes.

Thus, whether Venus is presented as a malefic or a benevolent force seems to depend on who is speaking. Venus attracts the conflicting definitions of femininity that often come from seeing the feminine only as opposite or complementary to the masculine (the Mars principle).

Originally, the symbol of Venus came from the systems of astrol-ogy. It is now used in biology to indicate the female and is a wide-spread and accepted symbol, a sign often seen daily in modern culture, so a consideration of this symbol in depth should give our frequent encounters with it more depth, meaning, and resonance. First, remember Jones's initial definition of Venus as "a circle of spirit placed on top of the cross of matter." Aniela Jaffe says the Greek cross that gives weight and "bottom" to the symbol implies the mandala of earthy balance which gives gravity or *gravitas* to the spirit, helping to buoy it into a relationship with matter. Yet the symbol seems to me also akin to a Latin form of the cross, with the circle of self rooted downward into earthly completeness or, more negatively, the ego crucified on *materia* as a form in itself. The symbol also suggests the personality of woman transcending downward into mothering, especially the mother of an infant, whose ego is so bound up in caring for frail new life that it is truly transfixed, affixed, diminished, even crucified by the roots that the baby embodies. The cross also suggests an anchor that grounds women, keeping them from bounding free but also keeping them attached and connected.

Another and similar ancient image of woman is the vine that enwraps a tree, trading its beauty (flowers) and fertility (fruit) for male strength (the tree is barren without her). This is an image for marriage but also suggests the dependency of young mothers, their need for the protective shelter of a home and mate in order to thrive. Both the vine's roots and the grounding cross of ♀ insist upon gravity, (feminine "heaviness"), the downward piercing of physical density, the transcending downward in the feminine need for earth, for ground, to center on. Since the earth gives women spiritual values and a deeper understanding of their own bodies' processes, this rootedness is finally a foothold in a matriarchal spirit. Woman's experience of earth translates the earth herself into a true spiritual meaning.

Another natural image that has cosmic implications for women is the egg, which shows up especially in women's visual arts. Leona Carrington's most prevalent image is the egg. In "The Alchemist," she celebrates woman's biological and psychic fecundity, her power over life itself, with an egg at the feet of a sorceress and a red egg in the sky. In "The Alchemist," the oven transforms black primal matter, supposedly the least differentiated of matter, to gold, the highest essence of material reality; Carrington further ties the egg to the ovum, and she suggests that it is "through woman that humanity will ultimately be transformed and that psychic evolution will occur."[17] She writes of the egg in her work this way:

> This morning, the egg idea came again to my mind that I thought that I could use it as a crystal to look at Madrid, for why should it not enclose my own experiences as well as the past and future history of the Universe? The egg is the macrocosm and the microcosm, the dividing line between the Big and the Small which makes it impossible to see the whole. To possess a telescope without its essential half—the microscope—seems to me a symbol of the darkest incomprehension. The task of the right eye is to peer into the telescope, while the left eye peers into the microscope.[18]

The egg also appears in Remedios Varos' *La Llamda*,[19] in which a priestess strides forward with her hair spiraling into the sky and catching around a cosmic egg in the heavens. The ethereal flowing of her hair forces our eyes upward in the manner of Baroque painting, opening the viewer's vision to the cosmos. The priestess burns red with passion, power, and life and seems to warm the embryonic human figures emerging from the walls around her. In *Planta Insumisa* Varos has made her painting egg-shaped; it depicts a woman chemist who is creating plants; she is a fully conscious scientist, aware and careful of her shaping of biological forces. In *La Creacion de las Aves* Varos portrays an owl-woman who connects cosmic forces with the blood of her own heart to make living creatures, in this case birds that fly into the world. For Varos, then, the egg and blood are symbolic of women's cosmic connections.

A similar symbol important to women painters is the vulva. A good example is Judy Chicago's drawing called "Female Rejection Drawing."[20] The central symbol is a golden, key-shaped vulva; lines radiate from this sunlike center, suggesting an open framework. The strong primary colors of this painting radiate heat and suggest passion, energy, and power as central to the feminine principle. The center also resembles a lotus flower, an Eastern symbol of the most complex and advanced meditative state. This supports Alice Bailey's idea of Venus as the irrevocable, eventual unfolding and affirmation of the feminine principle which may be the key to ultimate love and connection with godhead.

This same sense of birth of self appears in a painting by Remedios Varos, *Luz Emergente*, which depicts woman giving birth to herself. A woman steps through a key-shaped opening made of parchment layers that peal away, suggesting an irrevocable opening by and of the female to reveal an essential mystery, which turns out to be feminine godhead.

Another symbol that seems helpful in understanding women's souls comes from lectures given by one of the most spiritual of Jungians, Tom Kapacinskas. He uses the Greek letter omega, Ω, to suggest the depth and mystery of the unconscious. The openness of the omega suggests an attitude of inviting receptivity to the mysteries of the universe. The omega's shape contains expansion and openness, a potent symbol for women, who see themselves not simply as containers but as images of stability that are open, receptive, steady.

Like the omega, women have an interchange between themselves and the depths of outer reality. Omega is the last letter of the Greek alphabet and has hitherto been claimed by Christendom as the image of God and of "last things," such as the Apocalypse. Perhaps older men do connect into the flowing bonds of the omega, but older women represent the interrelated wisdom of fulfilled love. The old woman is an image of silent pondering and may connect with the fascination that certain women artists seem to have with mountains, which they see as very old women. In Gabrielle Roy's novel *The Hidden Mountain*, a young artist is caught in the throes of painting the essence of a northern Canadian mountain; Emily Carr, another Canadian artist, wrote movingly in her diary of her attempts to capture the essence of a mountain in her painting. Adrienne Rich wrote a wonderful poem "Phantasia For Elvira Shatayev"[21] in which she imagined the death of some women mountain climbers as a merging with the mother. Mountains, like the omega, suggest a silent, deep-rooted, ancient, and brooding psyche that cannot be fathomed but must be groped at by the mind.

Taken together, the symbols discussed in this chapter constellate powerful archetypes that could redeem humankind if allowed full manifestation. The omegas interconnect in a way that contains, receives, and gives light. Women who have established deep connections with other women find in this interweaving of perspectives a sense of a stable mother body as cosmos. The omegas interflow and give stability to the golden roots that intertwine beneath the earth and hold it together. Woman's physical fertility symbolizes her psychic fertility, her egg potential. If women can bring their Venus principle, their water, earth, and salt perspectives into public policy, into international politics, perhaps loving connections can soften and detoxify the hatred and bitterness that have brought our world to the brink of nuclear war.

10. Women's Spirituality and the Occult Tradition

A woman's spiritual development may follow paths within the patriarchal traditions of Judeo-Christianity that are, of course, still viable. In this chapter I present a list of other ways in which women can bring to consciousness their own internal imagery of self and womanhood rather than respond to and echo the projections of their culture.

Some readers will approach this chapter with deep-seated suspicions, prejudice, or even revulsion. Like Colette, they should suspend judgment and try to consider these images of spiritual reality as seriously as most people still consider official theology. No theology is any less someone's fantasy because it is collectively accepted. The occult traditions have been assigned to darkness, and as Jung often said, one does not become enlightened by imagining figures of light but by making darkness conscious.

Over the years I have found much meaning and consolation in the occult traditions. They have remained, however, a hidden element in my life, due to the contempt or anger that they generate. Sexist views of women's religious awareness have been so scornful, so bludgeoning, so smugly self-serving, that women generally speak of their spiritual life with great fear and reservation. Such male theorists and many of their female followers seem to fear that feminine mentality will destroy all rationality, all distinctions, unless it has a masculine superego to control it. For instance, James Hillman discusses the danger he sees in matriarchal values:

Without the father we lose also that capacity which the Church recognized as "discrimination of the spirits"; the ability to know a call when we hear one and to discriminate between the voices . . . but the spirit that has no father has no guide for such niceties . . .[and] puts an end to spiritual discrimination; instead we have promiscuity of spirits (astrology, yoga, spiritual philosophies, cybernetics, atomic physics, Jungianism, etc.—all enjoyed currently), and the indiscrimination among them of an all-understanding mother.[1]

His use of the word *promiscuity* labels the feminine ability to hold various contradictory beliefs in an easy tension as whorish. He fears a descent into chaos and, like others of his kind, puts studies on witchcraft, astrology, parapsychology, reincarnation—seen as inferior systems of thought—into one box under the label "occult."

A more current reason for the rejection of parapsychological studies is the pseudopsychology of the academic quantifiers, especially the new breed of psychologists. Arthur Koestler has devoted a book to parapsychological phenomena, which he says modern psychology ignores to its and humanity's peril. He sees much of the current prejudice as issuing from the dominating school of behaviorist psychology:

> The professor of psychology at McGill University, D. O. Hebb, a leading behaviorist, frankly declared that he rejected the evidence for telepathy, strong though it was, "because the idea does not make sense"—admitting that this rejection was "in the literal sense just prejudice." The mathematician Warren Weaver, one of the founders of modern communication theory, was equally sincere: "I find this [ESP] a subject that is so intellectually uncomfortable as to be almost painful. I end by concluding that I cannot explain away Professor Rhine's evidence, and that I also cannot accept his interpretation."[2]

Two recent letters to the editors of *Psychology Today* provide a gloss for this attitude. One points out that "behaviorism, with its tendency to treat an individual as an object to be molded into conformity, is tied with right-wing thinking." The other letter defends behaviorism because it insists that only environments, not people, are bad, but goes on to say that "hardcore behaviorists themselves tend to be among the most conservative people in psychology."[3] Dogmatic, exclusivist, materialistic—American psychology fosters qualities that naturally recoil from the spiritual implications of parapsychology.

Perspectives that force theories of human personality into greater complexity are anathema to such researchers. Yet occult fantasies of reality are certainly richer and more reverential to the human soul than what any school of psychology now provides. So again, adopt Colette's accepting skepticism. Whether auras, reincarnation, and clairvoyance are objectively true can probably never be discovered as we move in this finitude of flesh. Putting the possibility of truth aside, what kind of positive theories of the feminine do we find in these bodies of thought? What is the meaning of gender in this metaphysics? Do these traditions reflect more of the feminine than the more official ones do? Are there richer ways to see what we as women do, which these traditions offer? Can we augment and illuminate our growth further from these perspectives?

Many women are believers in astrology. In 1963, the French Public Opinion Institute published the results of research into national attitudes about astrology:

> The results were used to draw a "profile" of the typical astrologer's customer. She is a young woman between twenty-five and thirty, of good education and above-average income. She is mainly interested in her personal future, but is also concerned with predictions about world politics.[4]

In my classes, I offer to obtain my students' natal horoscopes as another slant on their personalities, to supplement the Myers-Briggs typology test and other personality tests. I always explain the underlying difficulties with tests and urge skepticism as students try each system as a mirror or focus. Several women students from each class have availed themselves of this offer, but not a single man has done so.

There are many reasons that astrology might appeal especially to women. Comparing charts is a way to know one another more quickly; women discuss where Venus is in a chart in order to explain their love relationships, or they discuss their moon positions as a shorthand for understanding hidden moods. Further, astrology may be a helpful system of personalizing the forces of God within and without. Astrology fleshes out interconnections between psychic forces; it interweaves forces in a way natural to the feminine psyche. Also, any chart can be interpreted an infinite number of ways; there are probably more approaches to astrological readings than there are modern psychological schools. This too appeals to women. The moment that an astrologer emphasizes one force — say, fire — she can also show how it is influenced by another force in the chart, so that the client's psyche is allowed much imaginative flow and connection between opposites.

Astrology provides a cosmology of friendly, relativistic forces, all of which impinge on personality formation at the moment of birth in each person. So it is a way of talking about interconnections between people, too. I have heard women discuss intensely their relative sense of the importance of children because of which planets fall into the house of children. Finally, the natal chart itself, when drawn in different colors, is an aesthetic object—a mandala that names the spiritual forces within each of us and through which we can focus on self and meditate on our significance in the cosmic order of things.

All fields have their jargon, and I find the mythological and planetary language of astrology more beautiful than the positive reinforcements of behaviorism, the anal/oral orientation of Freudianism, or the shadow and archetype of Jungianism. Astrology is one way of getting back to "story" in its primordial form.

It is important to note here that some astrologers are as sexist as the worst Christian fathers; one modern astrologist, Ted George, for example, postulates a yet-undiscovered planet, Persephone, as a positive feminine influence on the natal chart, but then goes on to name nine also unknown dark moons who are the "sisters of evil," including

> EDITH: This is the power of the body over the mind.
> It is the temptress of the flesh.
> MARTA: The sister of greed.
> BETTIS: A destroyer of good thoughts. This is the sister to beware of most of all. She will do more destruction than all the others.
> LYSTRA: This is the evil woman in a person's life.
> FREDA: Represents the filth of the body and mind.[5]

Persephone and the nine dark moons are yet another rendition of the Madonna/Whore, Mary/Eve dichotomy; note especially the moons' evil physical aspects. George's fantasy multiplies the Weird Sisters by three and projects the Seven Deadly Sins as a troupe of cosmic women, a horde ready to attack. Yet, in the American tradition of self-contradiction, he is pro-abortion and pro-feminist in other ways.

Before moving to another topic, I want to emphasize that theories of astrology are extremely complex; there are infinite numbers of approaches to a natal horoscope and great disagreement among astrologers on how to read certain aspects. There are so many relationships to be read within a chart that it is truly inexhaustible, so that no final word can ever be settled on. That, I think, is as it should be.

REINCARNATION

For a number of years, I have been reading reincarnationists to see what light they can shed on the question of the meaning of incarnation in a female body. My chief source is Ian Stevenson; he has investigated many cases throughout the world of children (usually under five) who apparently remember previous lives, speak foreign languages learned in those lives, and so forth. He reports that there were differences in sex between the present and antecedent personalities in fewer than 10 percent of the six hundred cases he investigated. In one case study, he remarks that in two such incarnations, the individuals showed discomfort at the typical behavior of their gender. One was a boy in his present incarnation, and seemed to have developed a definite preference for female roles. His mother, his schoolteacher, and others testified to this. The evidence consisted of a marked preference for the society of girls, a skill and intense interest in sewing, a fondness for silk shirts and, on occasion, painting his fingernails.[6] The child who was a girl in her present incarnation showed some tendency toward masculinity: "Gnanatilleka said to her parents quite simply, 'I was a boy. Now I am a girl.' On the day of [Stevenson's] visit to Medunawewa, she said when she had been a boy, she had wished to be a girl. When asked whether she was happier as a boy or as a girl, Gnantilleka replied that she was happier as a girl."[7] In some cases, the individuals who have different genders from those in their previous lives never marry, living quite happily as celibates.[8]

Stevenson seldom draws conclusions in his work, but he implies that some individuals, perhaps 10 percent of the population, are simply not comfortable in the gender of their bodies. It is interesting that recent research on homosexuality, a definitive study from the University of Indiana, presents findings that 10 percent of the population is homosexual. Perhaps bisexuality and homosexuality reflect natural sexual orientations of souls who have taken on specific gender identity or gender problems throughout the ages.

Stevenson's research also implies that many souls take on the same gender over and over and that they tend to prefer reincarnating in the same racial group. The lives he reports on often seem quite similar from one life to the next. In a way the process and theory of reincarnation suggests and affirms the possibilities of infinite time, which allows time for the simple accretion of experiences in many obscure lives. Stevenson's more recent research has discovered some cases of corrective "demotion," when a previous life was dissolute or cruel, which suggests that perhaps we do live in a balanced and just universe.[9] A consoling hope.

More important to my theory of feminine personality, though, is the idea that 90 percent of all women have been women in more than 90 percent of their several lives. To most reincarnationists it is clear why a soul would prefer to take on a female form over and over:

> Women were immensely important in the early days of the earth, as they are today, for they are blessed with the creative force of the universe and are, therefore, nearer to our Creator than those who have the seed but are helpless to propagate without the womb of woman. She it is who carries the egg to be fertilized, and gives of her own body to bring forth the temple for another soul to occupy . . . the so-called Curse of Eve — menstruation and childbearing — was the highest blessing the Creator could bestow on his beloved souls: the power of co-creating with himself . . . God himself is totally whole, being neither male nor female, and the only reason Jesus spoke of God as 'Our Father' was to conform to the customs of the times . . . eventually the pendulum will swing back and woman will again take her rightful place on an equality with man.[10]

Another reincarnationist says that women have greater intuition and sensitivity than men and that womankind needs to accept more "totally its energetic role," and bring this energy into the world at large:

> To do this properly, women have to come into their own, they have to release their full potential as human beings, and so make a balance

between the matter aspect and the spirit aspect on this planet—I'm talk-ing in terms of energy—and when this takes place, you will have Masters in female bodies. [11]

This same writer has a mediumistic dialogue with a disincarnate prophet who reports that the family unit must be retained for in-coming souls, but that it must be expanded into the community. This prophet points out that the isolation of the nuclear family is an artificial thing and that the apparent breakdown of the institution of the family is really a gradual extension of "our allegiance and our identification from the family to a larger group, from the larger group to the community, from the community to the community of nations."[12] The importance of the family as a civilizing force to which women are central is explicit here, but also there is a visionary hope for the merging of the family and community in a way that will free women from total envelopment in family life.

The literature of reincarnation often opposes more traditional Western views of the housewife or mother as a less-developed being; the family and home are described rather as a crucible for individua-tion or for the evolution of the soul. Edgar Cayce always spoke of marriage and family as a reflection of the most ultimate harmony, to be sought after by both sexes:

> Do make the home your career, for this is the greatest career any soul can make in the earth. To a few it is given to have both a career and a home, but the greatest of all careers is the home, and those who shun it, shall have much yet to answer for. [13]

Following the Alice Bailey tradition that large groups at times reincarnate to accomplish specific social goals, here is Benjamin Creme, another mystic:

> So the family is essential. We choose our families. We don't choose a group; we are part of a group. We incarnate as groups and choose the father and the mother, which is our family, who will provide the body which our soul, our true self, sees will give the approximation in vibra-tional rate, and opportunity, therefore, to the kind of level which we as souls are evidencing, at any given point, as we incarnate. [14]

It is possible that strong women from all past cultures are coming together as a group now and incarnating to give impetus to the raising of human consciousness through a relatedness, an emphasis on *eros* to counter the *logos* of previous cultural development. Perhaps the reason so many brilliant women find their footing later in life and are so apparently uncomfortable in their younger bodies is that they are old and highly evolved souls. Reincarnation theory has it that old souls are restless and limited in young bodies, where social and biological individuation has not yet caught up with actual wisdom and intellectual depth.

REINCARNATION AND ABORTION

Because the issue of abortion rests so much on when the soul becomes one with the body, it is interesting to see how reincarnationists handle the idea. Gina Cerminara, a writer on reincarnation, interprets Cayce's data as saying the soul can enter the body shortly before birth, shortly after birth, or at the moment of birth: "As much as twenty-four hours can elapse after an infant is born before the soul makes entry, and in some cases, there are even last-minute changes with regard to the entity which will enter."[15] Cayce even advises that mothers give care to their thoughts during pregnancy as they will attract certain types of entities to them: "If you wish a musical, artistic entity, then think about music, beauty, art. Do you wish it to be purely mechanical? In that case, think about mechanics—work with such things."[16] This does not negate the spirit which animates the fetus during the whole pregnancy, the spirit which apparently responds to the heredity of the developing body, and which Cayce differentiates from the late entering soul. Stevenson urges that psychologists look to heredity for family resemblances and proclivities, but consider reincarnation for differences between family members.[17]

Joan Grant, a major writer on reincarnation, thinks the soul interested in later inhabiting the fetus chooses which genes should be dominant or recessive and then watches over the mother as she moves toward birth.[18] Reincarnationists see the body as a vehicle, a channel, that is appropriate for and hence attracts or even is shaped by an incoming soul. Rather than a sin or wrong, astrologist Ted George sees abortion as a favor to a soul who would otherwise face development in a difficult environment:

> Voluntary abortion is facilitated by spirits. The decision to do such is placed in the mind of the mother by spirits . . . it is better that the child

and the soul not be born. For this reason, abortion is not wrong. If the soul were born, it would not fulfill its incarnation and thus be penalized further. The decision for voluntary abortion is not an easy one. But having given birth to a new soul when it is not really wanted increases the burdens for the soul to bear which can result in far more serious consequences. [19]

Probably the most helpful advice I have found for a woman who feels guilty after having an abortion comes from a medium through whom an entity called Cosmic Awareness speaks. This entity says that abortion incurs more guilt when no birth control has been used, but tells how even then karmic debt (translate as guilt) may be alleviated:

This Awareness indicates that a violation by one who negligently leaves the door open, or the one who consciously entices by opening the door constantly and carelessly, and under such seductive influences and attitudes as would surely bring someone in, then consciously and violently rejecting: this kind of violation brings on greater karma than the one who negligently allowed someone to enter and with much regret and sorrow felt forced to have the entity removed.

This Awareness suggests the sensitivity felt toward the entity as that which alleviates much of the karma. The hostility sent toward that entity with the attitude of "get it out of here" is that which can bring on greater karma. This Awareness indicates the alleviation of karma is through responsibility and communication. But wherein one is irresponsible, then communication with that entity who enters into your home must be such that the entity does not feel great hostility at being rejected . . .

This Awareness indicates that many mothers allow their children to enter without condition, and in due course find themselves having no life of their own and their children being the dominating force in their life, and themselves simply responding and reacting to the commands of the child: the cries, the tantrums, the moods, the demands. This is likened unto being so foolish that you not only allow the door to be open to invite the stranger, but you also allow the stranger to enter and take over your house, and perhaps even eventually eject you from your house and have the stranger taking over all that you held sacred, as simply flaunting it as an inheritance of no value . . . in allowing entities into your home, you may bring forth certain rules, certain regulations, certain conditions which can create the space for them to be and not hinder your own space for you to be. [20]

This emphasizes that the mother's first responsibility toward human individuation is to herself; she must look to her own soul's growth before she invites into her space another entity for whom she will be responsible.

While I am certainly pro-choice, I think the decision for abortion carries for most women a metaphysical dimension; most pro-abortionists are so afraid of the religious fanaticism of many anti-abortionists that they hasten to reduce the act to the level of pure physicality. Most women who have felt guilt even feel foolish and discuss their regrets and anxieties in a tone of shame. I think a good approach to a woman's pain or guilt is the concrete act of speaking to the soul that is to be aborted about her deepest and most positive feelings toward it. As Toni Morrison says, freedom means freedom to choose your responsibilities; to have an unwanted child, unless she plans to give it up, is irresponsible and perhaps "an escape from freedom" for the mother.

Besides providing guidance to women who face abortions, a medium can give very interesting information about past lives. Whether the past lives are true or the medium's personification of attributes she or he senses in the subject's personality is not important. This information can give a historical context to a person's sense of self, perhaps very necessary in a country as young as America, where ancientness is not a part of our heritage. The information that one has been of other races, the opposite gender, a child to one's own child in a past life is broadening to the sense of self and can stir the imagination into empathizing with others. It encourages a latitude of tolerance, a love of diversity for its own sake and for the richness that comes from complexity. This information prompts a person to consider the deep roots of antiquity and its infinite causality in our lives and actions, beyond our individual sight. It can give resonance to our relationships.

YOGA AND AURAS

Another non-Western idea that gives a helpful focus to women's problems are the spiritual levels symbolized by chakras. For women, the awakening and intensifying of the chakras can be especially helpful for intellectual and emotional focus and for shielding themselves from others' needs and feelings, which so often flood into their consciousness. In her reinterpretation of the Adam and

Eve story, Ruth Montgomery suggests how a person develops through the unfolding of each chakra; soul energy gradually works its way from the base of the spine to the top of the head and then above the head:

> The Garden of Eden, according to the Guides, was a figurative place located on no particular landmass, as the entire earth in the Adam-Eve days was green and verdant, without ugliness or barrenness. The snake was merely a symbol of the *Kundalini* (the creative power which lies coiled like a serpent at the base of the spine until awakened) and the forbidden fruit was the opening of the seven *chakras* (the psychic centers, or ductless glands) too suddenly, with the stress on the gonads (the earthly center) rather than on the pineal (the Christ center) and the pituitary (the master gland, or God force).[21]

Living in a state of original sin, then, is simply gathering too much energy in one center. One could see the first half of life for woman as centered more in the lower chakras up through the heart, which is especially developed in a nurturing or maternal life-style. The upper chakras of throat, third eye, top and out of the head, gain special force in the last half of life. Cosmic Awareness concurs, stating its theory on menopausal symptoms:

> This Awareness indicates that the entire sexual circuitry as that which undergoes changes and this also in the hormonal balance in terms of the other endocrine glands of the body. This Awareness indicates essentially, what is occurring here is a shift from the emphasis of the lower, physical chakras to those of upper chakras, which becomes more emphasized during this period of life.[22]

Those who study the human aura say that women's auras vary with pregnancy, the onslaught of menstruation, and so forth. They also claim that women have wider, more oval auras than men, but with less distinct edges.[23] Perhaps this is why women are seen as a harmonizing force in a group; traditionally, the edges of their auras are less discrete so they intermingle more with others, plus reach out further in their surroundings than men's do. Some writers say that after a group of persons have been together for a time in some sort of meeting, they develop a group aura, all the auras flowing together, making the group one organism.

The structure of women's brains may be part of this greater empathy and group consciousness. Recent research shows that "the celebrated female advantage in discerning the emotions of others seems to arise in part because women use both hemispheres of the brain to understand emotion, while men rely primarily on the right."[24] This researcher says that women can respond to verbal codes or labels plus imagery codes such as visual imagery or voice tones; he says that women have "ambidextrous brains." Thus empirical data support the aura theorists in suggesting that women see and hear a broader spectrum of data in dealing with relationships.

Some writers say that the female aura is generally both larger and better developed than the male: "The rays seem capable of being influenced by the will of the person possessing them and it will be found that women are able to project them from any part of the body, or even to change their colour."[25] Thus, even the shape and form of the female aura suggests that a woman innately has great spiritual force and hence also a pressing need for spiritual focus and discipline.

Everyone will find her own path, but I have found Hatha and Kundalini yoga helpful. I can focus energy in the third eye (the chakra between the eyebrows that focuses the mind and will) when my body hurts me and control both the pain and my response to it. Lecturing to groups has always frightened me; centering energy in the throat (the speaking) and head (thinking and spiritual focus) chakras helps me to focus on the lecture as a serving function in my life rather than one in which my ego is so involved.

Because women are generally more empathetic than men are, they may need more specialized and conscious forms of protection from negative spiritual vibrations. Women need to learn to put up shields between themselves and the pathological, vampirelike needy or the viciously critical; learning to gather one's energy into the appropriate chakra can be almost life-saving in such situations. Also, meditating in a chakra in which a woman feels herself out of balance is a good way to turn within. For example, when I find myself becoming harsh or severely critical with others, I try to spend some time meditating in the heart chakra and blessing those I have most felt negatively toward. This may or may not be a form of self-hypnosis, but it works.

WOMEN'S PSYCHIC ABILITIES

Development of psychic abilities may be more natural to women's spirituality than to men's. There is some research that finds that even elementary-school-aged girls are consistently more psychic than boys. [26] A large number of junior-high-school children were tested, and girls were found to score beyond what was attributable to chance. The researcher subjected his data to many statistical analyses when this finding first appeared, and seems puzzled rather than challenged by his findings. He does not even guess at why these differences occur, preferring "to rest content with the contribution that widespread sex-differentiated tendencies in ESP scoring have been found, and turn research energy to richer fields."[27] Like many other researchers in this field, he substitutes statistics for thinking, almost as if he is fearful of delving into the meaning of his data.

Rhine, who does like to think, postulates that there is some heritable basis for marked ESP ability. He suspects that it is carried on the mother's side: "When I learned that the mother of a certain individual had possessed mediumistic ability, I rather expected to find a good subject in him and this judgement proved to be correct."[28] Members of both sexes in the family manifested this ability, but it was almost always apparent in mothers of the subjects. In later experiments, Rhine also found more ESP ability in children than in adults: "Adult results gave decisions that were *below* chance to almost the same extent that the deviations of the children were *above* chance."[29]

Though he found far more ESP in the matrilineal lines of his subjects and also in children, Rhine nevertheless guesses that ESP evolved for specifically masculine pursuits: "To the hunter, the warrior, the seaman — in fact, to nearly all life situations — E.S.P. might serve in many ways to give man an important margin of advantage over his enemies and his environment in general."[30] Yet ESP between mothers and children would clearly be of greater value to survival of the species, if one wants to wax Darwinistic. Perhaps the psychic mother teaches her child to listen to messages it picks up, or perhaps a mother becomes more psychic from dealing with children. Did early mothers of our species simply spend more time picking up subliminal clues as to dangers in the environment and nonverbal distress in their children, and so train their intuitive faculties to a greater extent than men did? Remember Colette's mother, Sido, standing in the center of her garden, vibrating with the messages that wind brought her.

Certain other research adds more implications to the subject of parapsychology and women. For example, when Osis and Carlson, two well-known experimenters in the field, tried sending moods to target psychics, the woman's moods were felt more by the psychics.[31] Some researchers say that specific quantitative laboratory research is antithetical to ESP performance, which is "highly dependent on the emotional loading of the target material."[32] Another reason quantifying techniques do not work well is that there is seldom a clear transfer of information but rather "a diffuse, symbolically encoded transfer of emotional contents and emotional states."[33] One researcher found that an informal setting was needed for a highly gifted female subject;[34] another study shows that the presence of aggressive, skeptical persons in the environment suppresses ESP in women, but not in men.[35] The more ego-involved the subject is, the less able she or he is to accomplish ESP "hits," the term for correct guesses in games of chance. This suggests that less ego-bound subjects, more in touch with their own unconscious and thus able to send out waves to others on an unconscious, emotional, moody level, are going to be more psychic.[36] It also suggests that women, being attuned to other people's moods as an aspect of their environment, can be very uneven in both their own moods and their psychic abilities.

The best article I know that summarizes the implications of such studies is Jule Eisenbud's "Some Notes on the Psychology of the Paranormal."[37] Eisenbud, a psychiatrist, traces the way in which, in a period of a few days, patients who did not know one another reflected each other's lives plus moods and events in Eisenbud's own life. He found himself acting as a sort of conductor of moods and symbols between people who did not even know of the others' existence; patients seemed to be reading events in each others' lives through Eisenbud, though he had no clue as to how this happened.

Like Eisenbud, too often "we are dealing with real people caught up in a web of envy, death wishes, guilt and remorse"—in other words, the amorality of the unconscious. At the end of his article, where he says that his findings are morally shocking and certainly frightening, he fears

> that the majority of my parapsychological confreres will hasten to join my psychiatric colleagues as they return to their safe and irreproachably sane statistics and elegantly contrived experimental designs; and these, I must say, for the most part could not succeed more brilliantly in keeping the paranormal from happening, in the best tradition of a long line

of sure-fire incantations and spells, than if they had been deliberately designed for such a purpose. [38]

In other words, one can hardly look to very many psychologists for help in really understanding or developing psychic abilities.

The best psychics have always given us the most helpful advice for finding truth: look within. There are many techniques for this. Besides yoga, the method that Enid Hoffman outlines in her book on Kahuna is one way to develop a dialogue with your inner soul and to learn to listen to your intuition. [39] Hoffman tells how to find out the name of what she calls the lower self (most psychologists would call it the unconscious). Then she explains ways to communicate with the lower self which, as she rightly asserts, we ignore to our peril. She explains how to use the swinging of a pendulum to listen to the lower self: the lower self will use the body's positive and negative charges to make the pendulum gyrate in a way that signals yes, no, maybe, good, bad, and so on. This is a good way to focus on a problem, to try and keep it within the perimeters of one's own being.

Another helpful way to develop one's own inner imagery and to allow scope to the imagination and passions is to use Active Imagination to finish your dreams in a group, such as Naomi Goldenberg suggests in the last chapters of *The Changing of the Gods*. [40] To exercise Active Imagination, a person closes her eyes and lets a dream proceed on, as if she were watching a film; usually the person relaxes first so that ego-consciousness will become passive, a viewer, not a controller. Goldenberg describes ways in which a dream can be dreamed onward: the dreamer closes her eyes, relaxes, and lets her imagery respond to the questions of the group of persons with her. In this way a dream can become collective, too, as the questioners interact with symbology.

The Progoff Intensive Journal workshops also provide a way to focus on the many aspects of one's life and relationships. The journal given out in the first workshop has many sections for meditations on such topics as important persons in your life, and invites you to write biographies and consider landmarks in their lives; then you add significant interactions in this log throughout your life. Another section is for an ongoing dialogue with the body as it changes its instructions and limitations throughout life. Like the natal horoscope, the divisions provide a mandala-focus on life.

Such ancient occult traditions as numerology or the use of the *I Ching* are also helpful to many women. Your particular feminine typology will decide which techniques are the best for you.

POLTERGEISTS

A strange evolution apparently now occuring in the spirit world possibly reflects social changes. The population of poltergeists (and their agents) is shifting from predominantly female to male, and the psychological nexus is different, too.

Poltergeists are spirits that attach themselves to a particular place or person and cause incongruous disturbances, knocking things off shelves, tipping over chairs, and so forth. They are generally negative, destructive spirits, opposite to the spirits said to surround us and channel good, ennobling forces through our most positive sides. Some occultists say that we have a conglomerate and constantly changing group of spirit guides. In his fascinating *The Little Book of Life After Death*, Gustav Theodor Fechner describes how this works:

Man does not often know from whence his thoughts come to him: he is seized with a longing, a foreboding, or a joy, which he is quite unable to account for; he is urged to a force of activity, or a voice warns him away from it, without his being conscious of any special cause. These are the visitations of spirits, which think and act in him from another centre than his own. Their influence is even more manifest in us, when, in abnormal conditions (clairvoyance or mental disorder) the really mutual relation of dependence between them and us is determined in their favor, so that we only passively receive what flows into us from them, without return on our part.

But so long as the human soul is awake and healthy, it is not the weak plaything or product of the spirits which grow into it or of which it appears to be made up, but precisely that which unites these spirits, the invisible centre, possessing primitive living energy, full of spiritual power of attraction, in which all unite, intersect, and through mutual communication engender thoughts in each other, this is not brought into being by the mingling of the spirits, but is inborn in man at his birth . . .

So when man has entered into life other spirits perceive it and press forward from all sides and seek to add his strength to theirs in order to reinforce their own power, but while this is successful, their power becomes at the same time the possession of the human soul itself, is incorporated with it and assists its development.

The outside spirits established within a man are quite as much sub-jected to the influence of the human will, though in a different way, as man is dependent upon them; he can from the center of his spiritual being, equally well produce new growth in the spirits united to him within, as these can definitely influence his deepest life; but in har-moniously developed spiritual life, no one will has the mastery over another.[41]

Poltergeists seem to be spirits who cannot give up this plane of existence, even though they ought now to reside in the spirit world. Typically, poltergeist agents (the living people to which the spirits are attracted) have been female; the famous sixteenth-century case of an eighteen-year-old nun who attracted a dead, criminal nun has the usual earmarks of traditional poltergeist phenomena. Very often the agent is an adolescent and feeling a great deal of sexual confu-sion. As Fechner points out in the quote above, the spirits gain control over their human counterpart only when abnormal condi-tions allow them to dominate. I have heard psychologists describe adolescence as a time of schizophrenia because so many sides of the personality are struggling to emerge and often contradict each other, so it seems logical that poltergeists would attach themselves to adolescents. Also, the fact that until recently the agents were usually female can be ascribed to the greater sexual repression of female children in adolescence; the more permeable ego membranes of girls also possibly have made them tools for this kind of spirit.

The more usual case today is of a male agent, young, often living with persons other than his parents, and invariably harboring re-pressed aggression. Poltergeists set more fires than they used to.[42] Is male aggression more prone to conflagration (fire, sulfur, air)? Are there more displaced young males now than before? There are many possible interpretations, but the data are tantalizing. It will probably take many years of investigations to see more patterning in these phenomena. But it is delightful to think that the emancipation of the feminine body and spirit is having an effect even on the other side.

MOTHERING FROM BEYOND THE GRAVE
One beautiful theory that comes out of spiritualism is that the mother-daughter relationship never dies, at least where it was a close and rewarding one in life. We all remember the touching moment in

Jane Eyre when the heroine prays to her dead mother at a confusing juncture in her life. Jane receives the guidance she asks for. In much the same way, Harmon H. Bro spends the first portion of *Edgar Cayce on Dreams*, in showing how a young woman named Frances received messages from her dead mother in her dreams. Some of the dreams concerned medical advice, even advice on purchasing clothing. The mother's spirit entered into Frances's dream life, especially during pregnancy; during the actual labor, Frances claimed to have seen her mother, and her husband wrote that he too felt and was influenced by the mother's presence. The underlying basis of this young mother's relationship to her own mother is the theme of the following dream:

> Said my mother: "Your sister-in-law will be all right. We are all working for her recovery here." Then said someone else, or my mother, "Yes, that is the trouble. We cannot do what we want to do—go on and develop, because we still have dear ones on earth that need our help. This keeps us close to earth. We have to always be looking after you young people."
> Later, my mother showed me this latter in emblematical fashion, showing me how the mother love I have for my baby survives in the spiritual individuality of a cosmic entity, as for example it does in her for me. Thus she gave me another lesson of the life after death, and of all life, love and close relationship of loved ones—of life's greater joy and glory depending upon service. It was as follows: I was preparing to go home to Mississippi, where I wanted to go. I was saying good-bye to all and my mother was packing my trunk. Seeing my baby, I changed my mind about going and stayed with my baby. Just so, my mother, loving me, her baby, stays close to earth with me, although the freedom of the universe holds an alluring invitation for the application of her present spirit power. [43]

Cayce told Frances that "the time would come when the mother would move on, along her own soul's path of growth. For the present, Frances could count on her steady help." [44]

Frances's relationship with her mother followed the Demeter/ Persephone pattern, but Eileen Garrett, probably the greatest female medium that ever lived, tells of how a mother will return simply to protect small children who cannot fend for themselves. She was called in to talk to a poltergeist who was plaguing a farmer, his two young sons, and their stepmother. The dead mother accused the stepmother and the farmer of taking the sons' inheritance and of plotting her death; the young stepmother broke down, admitting everything.[45] Garrett also tells how Cecil B. De Mille's mother returned to chide him for all the bathtub scenes in his movies and to upbraid him for not making more meaningful films.[46]

Several years ago, I had the strongest impressions of my grandmother, dead many years; images of her came during meditation, and several months later a medium told me that she visits my home regularly to see how I am doing. Interestingly, in my images of her (mental images, not hallucinations) she no longer had white hair, but rather had the bright red hair and a youthful appearance that I never knew.

Interestingly, the only dead father Garrett ever mentions returned because of jealousy and hatred of his wife; he apparently manifested by his killing his wife's dogs through his angry young daughter — hardly a loving connection. Of course, we have the return of Bishop Pike's son[47] and of Ruth Plant's brother,[48] both very young men when they died. Their messages appear more general and less personal, however, than do most mothers'.

Maternal love that goes even beyond the grave suggests the depth of the bonds of mother love and seems to validate Eric Erikson's stress on the first stage of life as the time when one learns primal trust. When Hans Küng spoke in Kalamazoo, Michigan in October 1981, he discussed the insanity of those who have faith in God with no trust, no belief in real persons. He claims that Erikson's first stage is antecedent to all true faith. Those who care for the very young lay the bedrock for their adult metaphysics. In this vein, he said an atheist can have more basic trust and confidence in the world, more faith, in short, than a member of the clergy. Since most daughters are closer to their mothers than most sons are, and since that closeness means that a daughter watches her mother grow and individuate into old age, women's primal trust must be more extensive, intricate, and more dynamic than men's.

In sum, it seems likely that women are more psychic than men are all their lives, and that they resist these interconnections considerably less than men do. In *Spiritual Midwifery*, Gaskin tells of births that were preceded by extrasensory perceptions in either herself or the mother as to special medical care the infant would need as soon as it was born. A woman doctor, Michelle Harrison, also recounts dreams that made her take special precautions to save lives of mothers and babies; she says,

> I am more comfortable with my dreams about childbirth now. I don't try to ignore them nor do I automatically act on them. They are simply one more bit of information in an area that is usually uncertain, indefinite, and the result of complex interactions among the people involved, both those of us who have already been born and those of us still in utero.[49]

Even before birth, then, we may be in communication with our children; and our mothers seem even to reach back to us from beyond the grave. Women's connection to nature, their greater imbeddedness in process, may be read as a metaphor for their greater spiritual entwinement and merging with others, both living and dead. Matter, nature, this physical plane may after all be simply another aspect of the spiritual.

11. Morality and Matriarchal Wisdom: The Surfacing of the Goddess

I conclude with this chapter for two reasons. First, I believe that the ethics developed in this chapter and the metaphysics of the foregoing ones ought to be two sides of the same coin, that cosmology ought to imply right action, right reason. Second, I believe that the world badly needs matriarchal morality. If women's values and morals become part of public, governmental policies, women will make the world a more harmonious place for the human sojourn. With Robin Morgan,

> I want a woman's revolution like a lover. I lust for it, I want so much this freedom, this end to struggle and fear and lies we all exhale, that I could die just with the passionate uttering of that desire.[1]

If the values of the mothers prevail, the world will be safer for all living creatures — children, animals, plants, women, men.

THE MORALITY OF MEN

Lawrence Kohlberg first presented his six stages of moral development in his 1958 doctoral dissertation at the University of Chicago. He has continued his research in this area, gathering it together in a three-volume work, only the first volume of which, *The Philosophy of Moral Development* (1981), has been published. His scholarship and thought are important and solid. Every educator ought to read this book, which is shaking, passionate, and deserves better reviews than it has received. Kohlberg's veneration for the rational element of individuation, indeed his identification of highly developed rationality as individuation, comprises the best argument for *logos* as a form of *eros* that I have ever read. Yet his love for the rational faculty is often burst asunder by his underlying passion for justice. He envisions a better world and has a utopian vision of a world informed by educated reason.

One cannot quarrel with *The Philosophy of Moral Development* as a description of male moral development or for presenting a system of moral education especially needed for boys and men. The book is based on research done on boys and men. Kohlberg's methodology is unconsciously male-biased; his legalistic bent is centered in a male's experience of life; and his ideas for moral education omit the milieu in which most women develop and in which many still live out their lives.

Consider some of the questions he asked in his longitudinal study of boys in Chicago: Is an impoverished husband whose wife is dying of cancer justified in stealing the drugs that would cure her from a pharmacist who is overcharging for them? Should a judge give the husband the normal sentence for stealing? This problem elicited in younger boys lower-stage statements that husbands ought to care for their wives. To them, husbands "own" wives, and druggists (always referred to with the pronoun "he," which children always perceive as meaning a man) own the drugs; the argument is between two propertied males, each with certain things he wants to defend. Sexism becomes inextricably mingled with the lower-stage valuing of property, which often figures as more important than human lives. Furthermore, all Kohlberg's really serious life or death problems involve only male decision-making and situations. Perhaps it is impossible to ask questions that do not deal more with either female or male worlds than with universal, genderless issues, but researchers should address this issue before drawing universals from boys' answers.

These moral dilemmas from the world of male interests and dominion are probably balanced in Kohlberg's and his coauthors' minds by their two examples from the world of the feminine. One concerns a hypothetical young girl's choice between a new friend's and an old friend's invitations. The other concerns a real person, Andrea Simpson, a Quaker, whose despair came from her mother's death, her brother's insanity, "and her own failure to form a stable, intimate relationship with a man."[2] She felt that her life came to nothing and suffered a long period of depression. In her seventies she comes to an ethic of *agape* (spiritual love), which Kohlberg postulates as a possible seventh and highest state of morality.

> The religious orientation she evolved helped her to devote herself not only to her brother but also to other patients in the mental hospital where her brother was, for whom she developed programs, and to long-term efforts to improve race relations between blacks and whites. Her religious orientation, then, was an effort to integrate two forms of mysticism, the Eastern contemplative form and the Western form, which identifies inward spiritual union with God with active love for and service to fellow human beings.[3]

Note that neither of these examples involves legal systems, property or ownership, or the military. The guiding principles in both are the worth of certain relationships and persons. The girls' friendship problem was especially fraught with ambivalence precisely because it exists outside the legal domain.

Kohlberg's implicit metaphysical stance, which I think may be viewed as rather typical of many male theologians, is also a problem. Kohlberg claims to write from a "deontological" attitude, with no religious premises whatsoever, part of the attitude required for acceptance from his fellow social scientists. Yet he is a monotheist and a Platonist. He wants just one principle to define morality, and he overrides all others with it. He passionately believes that principled rationality, arrived at through cognitive restructuring of experience, will produce the highest form of morality, which he defines as the master virtue of justice. Even a casual reading of his stages discovers a Platonic ladder (reminiscent of the *Symposium*) that moves up and away from the concrete to more and more universal perspectives. Kohlberg would like to rid morality of its personal aspects, of its "content":

> I define morality in terms of the formal character of a moral judgment, method, or point of view, rather than in terms of its content. Impersonality, ideality, universalizability, preemptiveness . . . are the formal characteristics of a moral judgment . . . Moral judgments, unlike judgments of prudence or esthetics, tend to be universal, inclusive, consistent, and grounded on objective, impersonal, or ideal grounds.[4]

Kohlberg's emphasis on justice dovetails with a third aspect of his thinking that reflects his masculine approach to morality — his emphasis on legalism. Conflicting claims and conflict in general are central to his vision. He says he sees justice as the superior principle because it resolves conflicts. He stresses "reversibility," an ambiguous concept that seems to mean seeing the problem from the perspective of each person's rights. Even this role-taking principle is undoubtedly different for women and men; from the beginning girls often exhibit too much propensity to consider other people's rights more than their own. The theory also seems to presuppose that decisions are made between adults who can speak for their position, while many women deal mostly with children and their conflicting needs, not rights.

Kohlberg's constant concern with how his ideas of justice relate to judges and lawmakers is implicitly sexist. Women have not made laws, still do not make laws. Women judges and lawmakers are few and far between, and they work in a male-generated world. Women as the oppressed victims of a universal patriarchal system have usually had no recourse to defense of their desires or decisions as "rational"; rather, they have had to study the psychology of the dominant group (man the lawmaker) and figure out ways to manipulate and circumvent that group. Those women who followed the law often participated in the mutilation of themselves or their children, as elaborated in Mary Daly's *Gyn/Ecology*, which discusses footbinding, witch burning, and other official deaths and mutilations of women. Clytemnestra, in her ritual murder of Agamemnon after his sacrifice of their daughter, Iphigenia, is a fitting example of women's role. Agamemnon was of course obeying the law to placate the gods so that he could go to war, that all-hallowed masculine resolution of conflict. Aeschylus more than implies that Agamemnon (but not Clytemnestra) was absolved from murder because he was just obeying the law, just as people in modern culture continue to obey the implicit medical law that boy babies should be circumcised — a barbarism committed long before any sanitary excuses (all of which are under question now) were proffered.

My fourth objection to Kohlberg's theories is his choice of tragedy as the literature central to concepts of justice and moral development; this choice betrays a primarily masculine view of time as linear and ending in disaster. Kohlberg links self-actualization and joy, then says the fact of death destroys this. He says people should go to a mountaintop to be able to transcend this, while many women would find transcendent meaning in just the opposite, working and involved down in the valley where they are needed. His choice of Teilhard de Chardin as a theologian whose ideas support this theory also suggests a central sense of despair; Chardin's theology is centered on a despairing "prospect of a cosmic dead end"[5] that produces a desperate affirmation and love of the whole.[6]

A more typically feminine choice of literature that explains morality, justice, and cosmic patterns is the tragicomedy, which Shakespeare more or less invented to shape and contain his vision of life in his last years. In most of these plays, a daughter is lost because of the male protagonists' bad luck, misogyny, or impolitic decisions; life is affirmed many years later when the daughter, a redemptive Persephone figure, returns to the court, as does Perdita in *The Winter's Tale*. This is also the pattern in *Pericles* and, to a lesser degree, in *Cymbeline*. The feminine connection with the ongoingness of nature symbolizes the cycle of time which heals all wounds and introduces fresh forces into history.

My fifth point is probably more a cautionary note than an actual objection to Kohlberg's theories. I am convinced, with him, that education for morality is a desirable part of the public school curriculum; but if his theory is as based on male norms as I think it is, then once again little girls and young women will find themselves alien, jerked out of a natural development of the feminine ethics developed in their homes. I hope that researchers such as Carol Gilligan will continue to examine girls' and women's morality and find ways to integrate male and female development and the teaching of morality. Otherwise, yet another topic that will further support the patriarchal structure that underlies our culture will be introduced into the classroom. Since a preponderance of feminine ethics are taught by action and behavior of mothers, older sisters, aunts, and other older women, many of women's deepest moral attitudes are inculcated at a nonverbal level. For this reason it is hard for young girls and women even to name their discomfort at male morality, which comes so cloaked in words, rhetoric, and rationality.

Perhaps Kohlberg's hunt for a single path of virtue reveals not just a lack of intellectual generosity, or a desire to have the last word, or the play of a powerful mind carrying its thesis as far as it will go. His obvious pain over the plight of blacks in this country and over the Holocaust shows his deep metaphysical repugnance for the various political and legal systems that have produced such horror. In the depth of his unconscious he may realize how sorely masculine power needs to be harnessed; perhaps he feels that what he calls Socratic education toward justice will provide more super-ego strength to check masculine aggression. He seems to be thinking of this when he says, "We all know it is easier to think reasonably about physical matters than about moral matters . . . due to disruption by will, desire, and emotion in the moral realm."[7] But must even love be principled and rational?

SALT AND WATER: THE MORALITY OF WOMEN

Let us begin with philosopher Suzanne Langer's premise that a philosophy is only as good as the questions it begins with. I have asked quite a few women recently what the most significant and difficult moral decisions of their lives have been. The following examples are all from actual women.

1. A 32-year-old woman with two daughters knows that her ex-husband is verbally abusive with the children and confuses them. He refuses to pay child-support money, and one side of her would like to refuse his visits for this reason. She worries the whole time the children are with him because he does not watch them as closely as he should; they are quite young. In spite of all this, the children are attached to him and would suffer if she did not let them see him. Should she continue to do so? Either way, damage is done to the children.
2. The father of a sixteen-year-old girl has made sexual advances toward her. She loves her father and does not want to alienate him and lose his affection. To tell her mother might break up an already shaky marriage, and her mother is ill and might not be able to bear the stress. No matter what the girl does, irreparable damage and loss will be inflicted either on her or her family structure.
3. A woman has enough money to support her grandchildren, who are actually hungry sometimes because her son, their father (a college professor), refuses to give enough money to

their mother, who has no marketable skills, is very timid, and cannot defend herself against her husband's tyrannical miserliness. If the grandmother gives money to the mother, however, the husband will take all or most of it and use it on records, drugs, alcohol, and other things for himself.

4. A woman with a teenaged son has remarried; she becomes pregnant owing to the failure of her IUD. Her son is desperately troubled over his biological father's rejection of him and yet cannot accept his stepfather, whom he sees as usurping his mother's love. She feels that having another baby at this time might deepen her son's sense of rejection and that he may never recover. Yet she would like to have the baby and has a personal abhorrence for abortion. Should she have the baby, which would also interrupt her career and complicate her new marriage?

5. A woman divorces her second husband. Several years later, when the daughter of that marriage is twelve and the daughter from her first marriage is twenty-three, the oldest daughter becomes suicidal. The mother discovers that her second husband sexually assaulted the older daughter during two years when she was age twelve through fourteen. He threatened to kill her if she told. The second daughter seems to have a good relationship with her father and is deeply attached to him. All literature on incest says that men who do this generally go straight down the line of available children; if this man committed incest with his own daughter, chances are she would not tell because she would be afraid that her mother would refuse to let her visit him. The younger daughter is an emotionally frail child and would suffer greatly if cut off from her father. On the other hand, incest has made the older daughter practically unable to relate sexually with men her own age, an emotional block that causes her to feel suicidal. What should the mother do?

6. A woman is married to a man who will not give her enough money to feed their five children. He is also prone to erratic and violent outbursts, so she and her children live in fear. She is afraid to leave him as she has no job skills and she thinks the children would be worse off, perhaps living in the streets and on welfare.

This last case is a modern echo of women throughout patriarchal time, living under legal systems in which the father owns the children, though in modern times the ownership comes through the man's greater training in job skills and hence his ability to provide for the family in financial ways. Roman and Victorian women usually had no choice but to stay with brutal husbands; they wanted to protect the children, who legally had to stay with an abusive father and would have been even more vulnerable and bereft without their mother. A single Roman woman could procure an abortion, but a married woman could not because as soon as she married, her fetus belonged to her husband and the state. The current move in this country to phase out abused-spouse shelters is an attempt to return women and children to the same status of chattel. The law and justice have hardly been synonymous for women.

The characteristics of these dilemmas to some extent obviate even the possibility of a moral decision. Whether to steal drugs to save a dying spouse—would that all moral decisions were so simple and straightforward. The consequences of such an act are clear and immediate. The consequences of women's decisions often can only be guessed at, and whatever they are, they cannot be evaluated after years, if ever. Moreover, women cannot make decisions "formalistically," but must make them in the context of personal evaluation. In case 4, the mother is going to have to decide whether to abort on the basis of her evaluation of her son's psychic strength to bear up under another displacement of parental affections. Kohlberg's analytical method of Socratic dialogue can hardly resolve the issue.

Probably some questions cannot be answered from a "moral" basis, and that itself should be part of moral education. This ambiguity is also precisely why laws cannot cover all situations; ontology varies from one person to another in a pluralistic society, and decisions should remain at a personal level. The best law in some cases would be a law that allows no law to be made. One cannot always apply a given principle to moral decisions. For example, look at case 5, where so many elements must be evaluated—the strength of the father/daughter bond, the possible increase in the father's maturity and restraint with his own daughter, the great emotional vulnerability of the daughter, the mother's hatred for what the father did to the oldest daughter.

Such dilemmas, mostly secret, wound and scar women's souls, warping their lives in ways that their communities will judge but never understand. For example, the girl in case 5 has recently learned that her older sister's insanity is probably linked to her father's sexual abuse. The elder sister will not leave her home and imagines that it is covered with animal feces; she cleans constantly and compulsively. She refuses to see a counselor. The woman in case 3 suffers anxiety and shame over her son's behavior, but hides the source of her pain from her friends, who only see her as an inexplicably troubled woman. The moral decisions that men make are more often open to the community, and so much more sympathy goes to men.

Women's decisions generally involve relationships in which their lives are inextricably involved. The results of their decisions will wrap around the very roots of their souls. All decisions that involve children and spouses are remade and requestioned, turned over and over, as the children develop and in different stages reveal the results of these decisions. Also, if one has children with a person, one never really divorces him or her. Because the mother is almost always the most deeply involved parent, she becomes, whether she wants to or not, a mediator between the child and its absent or visiting father, whose influence is often negative rather than positive. Thus the entanglements and snags of family love mire down, enmesh women's decisions. Judith Bardwick addresses this issue as power-fully as any writer I know:

> Marriage and thus family are where we live out the most intimate and thus powerful of our human experiences. The family is the unit in which we belong, from which we can expect protection from uncontrollable fate, in which we create infinity through our children, and in which we find a haven. The stuff of which family is made is bloodier and more passionate than the stuff of friendship, and the costs are greater too. [8]

Because so many of women's moral decisions are about intimate problems, women internalize their pain more deeply than men. Women have not spilled their pain onto others through war, rape, murder, assault; when they do vent it, it usually falls on their children, and then they doubly suffer to see how they have hurt those they most want to protect and cherish. Women's suffering, rather than the more masculine metaphysical despair, responds to the loss of the real and takes the form of ongoing grief that is muted and constant. One of the reasons women have not written much philosophy and theology is that they have simply needed less verbal explanation when they carry in their bodies the imprint of those unrealized and dead. Remember the dying protagonist of *Tell Me A Riddle*, who carries her dead son's being throughout her life. Women have always carried, borne, the heaviness of grief, a kind of knowledge of the womb.

Perhaps it is the indelible tracing of this maternal grief in the substratum of the female psyche that makes women able to face and nurse the dying, while men so often flee the face of even their most beloved when they are dying. From most ancient times women have had to fear and suffer the loss of infants whom they so passionately loved. To walk away from the child's last and terrible hours would be inconceivable to most women. Elisabeth Kübler-Ross documents a father's desertion of his family as a small daughter dies, yet the mother confers ardor and love on that child and her remaining child. The mother has been bereft of her support system, yet she goes on giving out of some incredible reserve of strength and endurance.

Over eons of time women have generally inherited and built on this innate female strength that endures and faces the darkest mysteries of human life. In *Tell Me A Riddle* the granddaughter is better able to accept and mediate death than her grandfather, a man three times her age. She is his teacher. Women perhaps need less verbal explanation of death than men, simply because they have seen so many of the dying through to the end.

A terrible aspect of feminine grief is infanticide. Midwives and birthing mothers themselves have smothered babies at birth. Some women privately grieve throughout their lives for abortions which they had no choice about. Another kind of grief that is yet to be explored and is not permitted public expression is that of the mother who put her baby up for adoption. In the last few years I have had several women students who have lived wounded lives since the legal adoption of their infants. Adoption has been found recently to create festering wounds of alienation in some of the children, but I suspect that many of the biological mothers grieve and suffer all their lives over these lost children.

An aspect of female history that is painful to contemplate is the murder of female infants when too many children were born. Some research suggests that in certain parts of France only one in ten females were permitted to live. It was a Holocaust that was visited on women for hundreds of years; and since they have been such a silent mass, it is an atrocity that has so far only been written on from the child's point of view. In these cases, the child is dead but the mother and sister siblings bear the wounds for life. The guilt of survival would be a heavy, open festering wound; undoubtedly surviving sons carried some of this onus too, but for the daughters it must have been deeper and stronger, a more internalized sense of guilt and also loneliness for those lost sisters. To individuate, to assert oneself, would seem risky to the living sister. Her life itself would seem a contingent favor. The grief that mothers must have repressed in order to get on with the tasks of caring for the living children should have split their psyche and lives in half, exploded them into millions of fragments. All of this has yet to be borne into historical consciousness; the feelings are still locked into and under statistics and historical archives. When men suggest that women do not laugh as often as men, when we are shown to be less playful, less "sports-minded," it may be because women have carried most of the grief of our species. This has been built into the structure of some cultures, who hire wailing women to follow a casket; the renting of clothes and tearing of hair has been an age-old symbol of grief enacted by women.

As a child grows older, parental grief over its death becomes more similar for the mother and father but even then is not identical. A mother's grief is, I believe, qualitatively different. The child is an intrusive/extrusive factor in a father's life, but an integral one to the mother, an extension of being that comes through her and remains part of her bodily awareness, a personification of her physical experience of carrying and birthing it. She responds to the child's physical needs as though they were an extension of her own body. To lose a baby is like losing her own arm or leg, a concrete part of her own body. The mother is central to the partitioning process of the generations; she is physically implicated when a child dies. For years doctors immediately removed a stillborn infant from the delivery room, trying to keep the mother from seeing it. Physicians have found that when they saw these mothers a year later, they were still grieving. Now the bereft mother is encouraged to hold the baby and say good-bye to it. They give up their grief more naturally and readily if they embrace the body of the lost child. (Consider here the pain of sons "lost" in war.) Mothers cannot pretend the child is only soul. It was certainly soul in *potentia*, but talk of the Resurrection is simply barbarously off the mark for the mother's experience of her child's death.

Talk of salvation is too abstract, meaningless, to account for the child's missing body, the reality of which the mother feels in her own body. Sometimes older women who have experienced this loss help the most, saying concrete, practical things like "Time will heal this and eventually you will be able to turn the grief off and on like a water faucet." Or "Don't fill your arms too soon or the new baby will suffer for the loss of the other." The naming and imaging of the pain, practical advice on how to live out its first stages—these are the most helpful and least reductionist ways of helping a mother through this.

WOMEN'S ONTOLOGY: THE *AGAPE* OF EARTH

Women's most typical forms of suffering issue from their bodies, and it is through the body that their natural theology comes. Women's ontology is based on a direct perception of the flesh, the immanent. If verbal thought and philosophy follow in the more intellectually developed woman, it seldom loses touch with its original birth in and through the flesh.

The intelligent and good mother is always operating at Kohlberg's sixth and highest moral stage, but modified, delegalized. She bases her dealings with vying siblings on the need of each to unfold in its own unique way. All good parents wrap mythic futures around the positive qualities they see in their children, and this helps each child to realize itself. Only the immature and less-developed mother sees her children as ego projections who must carry out those portions of her own unrealized being that she delegates to them. The good mother gives beyond what she can afford because she recognizes the great need in each child, which always calls for more than a mother knows herself able to give. She does not look to principles or legal systems to teach justice and fairness in that most constant and basic court of conflicting claims which constitutes sibling rivalry. (There is nothing like sibling rivalry to call forth the wisdom of Solomon.) She looks within herself and acts according to her intuition and the situation. She acts immediately because dispensing of justice will not await her deliberation. Children's needs are immediate and on the spot. Her perspective is that of a person who can be rational but recognizes that her charges are basically non-rational. She knows that teaching of rationality and justice is a long and arduous task, and learning it is lifelong, subsidiary to, and derivative of higher human values, such as love, tolerance, patience, and good will toward others.

When a mother reaches the end of parenting her own children, she becomes a grandmother or a matriarch to her culture, moving to a hypothetical stage seven. She moves beyond the personalism of investment in her own young, or, as in Andrea Simpson's case, beyond caring only for a beloved relative. *Agape* in whatever form goes beyond principles and ethics, and especially beyond one's biological roots — though for women it is usually rooted in an understanding of life and its values through their experience of family roles. *Agape* is qualitatively different from and higher than the justice that rests on the sterility and one-sidedness of analytical judgment. *Agape* is a more plenitudinous, reverential way of seeing things.

Truly to reverence life and its mystery is perhaps to give up trying to understand it with the rational side of the brain. Since women have more frequently moved through nonrational realms to arrive at this stage, we would expect their *agape* to be qualitatively different from men's also. Yet certain men apparently come to the same sort of wisdom. For Kohlberg, the man that most exemplifies the seventh stage is a perfect example of what I would call matriarchal wisdom. Janusz Korczak feared to have children because of insanity in his family and instead "adopted" thousands of Jewish and Christian orphans into schools he established in Warsaw. In the history of men, how many have taken a place with the destiny of their children with the passion and devotion of Janusz Korczak?

On the morning of August 6, 1942, German and Ukrainian guards surrounded the orphanage as part of the plan for elimination of "non-productive elements" to the Treblinka death camp. Prepared for death, Korczak led the 200 children from his own orphanage to the train station where the freight cars waited. Each child, neatly dressed and carrying a favorite doll or book, marched the two miles in a parade of quiet dignity. Korzcak lead the column, holding the two youngest by the hand. Stepha and the other teachers walked not far behind. His attitude toward his own impending death is expressed in two statements, "You do not leave a sick child in the night, and you do not leave children at a time like this."[9]

Kohlberg's example of stage seven, then, is a man who based the second half of his life on a vision of the sanctity of all persons, especially the young, of the Wise Old Woman, the grandmother of the species. Through his total identification with the children, Korczak was apparently able to mute his own pain and fear. Like Kohlberg's other seventh-stage example, Andrea Simpson, Korczak defined self through responsibility to others. His lifelong belief in the importance of children, even in his earliest years as a physician, when he wrote *How to Love a Child*, shows that a man can steep himself in feminine values and arrive at the same transrational conclusions.

What I am leading to here is that one of the great moral commitments women have always made is to their children, to the next generation. Erikson says "generativity," or caring for the young, is the last stage of morality (based on studies of men, of course); yet women's whole lives are generally spent on this. Not until the past forty years did many women outlive their youngest child's leaving home; women have not had the luxury of free will until very recently, because life was too hard for the vast majority. When a woman has a child, it is equivalent to taking life vows. That is the reason that Demeter is uncoupled in Greek myth, that Hestia and Artemis (originally in charge of childbirth, not hunting) are virgins.

Since historically most women found their individuation circumscribed by the role of mothering, let us examine some of the archetypal configurations and patterns this role has engraved on women's unconscious. For one thing, there is a maternal *agonistes* in the daily process of a child's growing up. I think women may place more value on adult life for the same reason that they may realize the expediency and necessity of ending life inadvertently conceived: to nurture and raise a human being properly takes the infinitely interruptable and constant attention of several adults, especially the mother. Perhaps because so few fathers have made their children their life work, they are able so casually to mobilize wars, institute capital punishment, burn widows on pyres, and so forth. Also, men are more easily able to make laws against euthanasia because they spend less time with the old, who would often embrace a way of dying at the close of a painful illness.

A woman yoga teacher who studies reincarnation told me that she believes souls reincarnate as mothers to burn off karmic debts more rapidly. Mothers' violent, intense experiences of the flesh are inexorable, deeply ingrained lessons in the labor of love. A mother's tasks work these lessons into the flesh and the psyche through their constant and repetitive nature. The cost of life is etched on a mother's very being.

There are certainly limitations to women's ability to serve constantly as caretakers. Women cannot always rise to the needs of their dependents. The current discovery of "granny" beating comes to mind here. This is the abuse of the elderly by their caretakers. It is interesting, however, that even in this case the women don't leave like men; many of the cases concern women caring for their mothers-in-law although their husbands have abandoned both of them. The women stay in the situation even though they sometimes explode into abuse. Women need very much to be alone, to enjoy a contemplative perspective in life, as they grow older. A woman trapped in the home with an old and helpless person has probably never had a job outside the home and so feels doubly trapped.

THE MATRIARCH AND COMPLETION

A certain passage in Jung's "Answer to Job" is a helpful introduction to a last image of the accomplished and achieved matriarch. In this passage Jung refers to the process of *enantiodromia*, when one archetype is too firmly constellated, its polar opposite automatically emerges, often forcefully and demonically. Too much light brings darkness; masculine perfection brings chaos if feminine completion is not allowed to coexist peacefully in balance with perfection.

Perfection is a masculine desideratum, while woman inclines by nature to *completeness*. And it is a fact that, even today, a man can stand a relative state of perfection much better and for a longer period than a woman, while as a rule it does not agree with women and may even be dangerous for them. If a woman strives for perfection she forgets the complementary role of completeness, which, though imperfect by itself, forms the necessary counterpart to perfection. For, just as completeness is always imperfect, so perfection is always incomplete, and therefore represents a final state which is hopelessly sterile. *"Ex perfecto nihil fit,"* say the old masters, whereas the *imperfectum* carries within it the seeds of its own improvement. Perfectionism always ends in a blind alley, while completeness by itself lacks selective values.

This arrangement [the Incarnation], though it had the effect of exalting Mary's personality in the masculine sense by bringing it closer to the perfection of Christ, was at the same time injurious to the feminine principle of imperfection or completeness, since this was reduced by the perfectionizing tendency to the little bit of imperfection that still distinguishes Mary from Christ. *Phoebo propior lumina perdit!* Thus the more the feminine ideal is bent in the direction of the masculine, the more the woman loses her power to compensate the masculine, ideal state arises which, as we shall see, is threatened with an enantiodromia. No path leads beyond perfection into the future—there is only a turning back, a collapse of the ideal, which could easily have been avoided by paying attention to the feminine ideal of completeness. Yahweh's perfectionism is carried over from the Old Testament into the New, and despite all the recognition and glorification of the feminine principle this never prevailed against the patriarchal supremacy. We have not, therefore, by any means heard the last of it.[10]

This passage not only reveals Jung at his most expansive and witty, but also shows how repelled he would have been at the way in which his followers have so simplified his ideas on individuation into simple "wholeness." Many women writers write of wholeness when what they really mean is full development of a particular woman's blueprint of self, a never-ending striving toward individuation on first this frontier and then that frontier of self. Growth ought to be an ebb and flow that seeks new channels, new shores. Wholeness suggests perfection, while growth suggests completion, a process that can go on even if parts are missing. Completion is fullness yet movement, tension. As Jungian psychiatrist and philosopher Jean Shinoba Bolen points out, the Tao path of becoming requires the foot as well as the head. The head must reflect on where the foot has gone.[11] It is more possible for women to find a satisfying completion by living an arduous life that serves others and hence interacts with others on a deep level than for a rich, spoiled woman or man to become whole by conceptualizing. The ideal of completion implies a restlessness, a movement, a deep engagement with the new enterprises and situations life presents. The life of self-indulgence produces a mushy softness.

The really mature matriarch reflects the dynamism of completion; she is salty, angular, sharp, especially if she has made her way through and survived terrible deprivation and disaster. Colette's mother was the mellowest of all the old women treated in this book, and in many ways she led the easiest, most contained life. Laurence, Morrison, and Colette all developed increasingly gnarled, longer, less coherent structures to carry their visions. This may reflect a sense that the last word is never in on anything. There is always something left over that could and maybe even needs to be added. The process of completion is often an increasingly intense demand to understand life, to take it all in and hold it in clear perfection, though only for an instant.

An essential ingredient keeps completion simmering, never-ending for women: the ongoing, constant assimilation of many sides of the feminine as carried by their friends, relatives, and lovers. Lesbian women especially enjoy and know deeply many women. As I suggested in my chapter on Colette, if one's mother is enculturated to assume only one face of the feminine, then the shadow side of that face appears. This reaching through the lover to the shadow side of the mother, even sometimes through memories of the actual mother to the transpersonal mother, places lesbianism within the confines of women's relationships to one another. In other words, the impetus that moves a woman toward her woman lover may be a desire to explore different faces of the Great Mother archetype, the feminine principle as embodied in different women, rather than a desire to move away from the masculine. Much theory in the past described lesbianism as a reaction to father, husband, brother, which makes her recoil from the "essential" and male rather than a positive seeking for her own feminine and unique path to completion. Some women who make their lesbianism a political as well as a personal choice may be remembering all their female forebears, the sadly thwarted matriarchs before them. Lesbianism may be on one level a re-membering of the feminine body both for the individual and her history.

Whether women's relationships have erotic bonds or not, the love that women bear for one another, the deep relationships that last all their lives, are central to the completion process of the matriarch's wisdom and morality. Sita is to Kate as Sula is to Nel as Francis Wingate is to Janet Bird as Mrs. Ramsey is to Lily. Women often love each other so deeply that even though they part, or one person dies, they carry the other woman within as the face of a previously undifferentiated side of themselves. The importance of women to each other is increasingly apparent as we become stronger and reach out to one another. It may be that the more women we know deeply, especially women different from ourselves, the more multifaceted will become our already fulsome, various points of view on justice and responsibility, what I have labeled our matriarchal morality. It is not by any means the older woman always teaching the younger woman. Consider how the middle-aged protagonist in Doris Lessing's *Summer Before the Dark* moves in with a very young woman and learns lessons about freedom. Venus, Demeter, Hestia, Hera—each an aspect of the domestic face of woman—have too long been polarized away from their Artemis sister; the home-oriented and the adventurous are beginning to learn from each other.

And so completion increases with a woman's immersion in the body of all women; the more that a woman can bring the symbolism of other women to a conscious level, the more she can enhance her own life and all lives around her with her ability to live out many sides of herself. There are the high points, instants of perfection in the process of completion. But matriarchal wisdom knows better than to make principle of them. We remember these epiphanies to re-member our souls and keep them moving.

Notes

Index

Notes

CHAPTER 1: Becoming an Adult

1. I have borrowed some of Carol Gilligan's language in summarizing Erikson's theory; see Gilligan, "Woman's Place in Man's Life Cycle," *Harvard Educational Review* 49 (November 1979), pp. 436-437. Otherwise I have adapted from Erikson; see Erik H. Erikson, *Identity: Youth and Crisis* (New York: Norton, 1968), pp. 94-95.
2. Nancy Chodorow, *The Reproduction of Mothering: Psychoanalysis and the Sociology of Gender* (Berkeley: University of California Press, 1978), pp. 161-162.
3. Erikson, *Identity*, p. 136.
4. Diane McGuiness, "How Schools Discriminate Against Boys," *Human Nature* 2 (February 1979), pp. 82-87.
5. Suzanne Langer, *Philosophy in a New Key* (Cambridge: Harvard University Press, 1957), pp. xiii, 5.
6. Recent anthropological writings confirm that most food in our ancestors' diet was gathered by women; see Frances Dahlberg, ed., *Woman the Gatherer* (New Haven: Yale University Press, 1981).
7. Ralph Mannheim, trans., and Erich Neumann, ed., *Amor and Psyche* (Princeton: Princeton University Press, 1956).
8. I borrow here from Jungian terminology; the "anima" is the man's image of women plus his expression of "feminine" traits such as tenderness, desire for relationship, feelings ahead of achievements. "Animus" means a woman's image of men and her expression of her own "masculine" traits such as aggression, achievement in the world outside the family, her drive to principled, logical thinking ahead of feeling-based decisions.
9. Erikson, *Identity*, p. 282.

10. Dorothy Dinnerstein, *The Mermaid and the Minotaur: Sexual Arrangements and Human Malaise* (New York: Harper and Row, 1976).

11. Margaret Laurence, *The Diviners* (Toronto: Bantam, 1974), p. 256.

12. Erikson, *Identity*, p. 265.

CHAPTER 2: Giving Birth as a Transpersonal Experience

1. Ina May Gaskin, *Spiritual Midwifery* (Summertown, Tenn.: The Book Publishing Company, 1977), pp. 282-283.

2. Karlis Osis and Erlendur Haraldsson, *At the Hour of Death* (New York: Avon, 1977), p. 64.

3. Stanislav Grof, "LSD Psychotherapy and Human Culture," *Journal for the Study of Consciousness* III (1970), p. 182.

4. Stanislav Grof, "LSD and the Cosmic Game: Outline of Psychedelic Cosmology and Ontology," *Journal for the Study of Consciousness* V (1973), p. 184.

5. Ibid., p. 184.

6. Ibid., p. 170.

7. Ibid., p. 172.

8. Ibid., p. 189.

9. Penelope Shuttle and Peter Redgrove, *The Wise Wound: Eve's Curse and Everywoman* (New York: Richard Marek, 1978), pp. 96-102.

10. Anaïs Nin, *Delta of Venus* (New York: Harcourt Brace Jovanovich, 1969), p. 163.

11. Grof, "LSD and the Cosmic Game," p. 174.

12. Ibid., p. 175.

13. One of the best and fairest modern meditations on the meaning of male sexuality is William O'Rourke's *Idle Hands*. The novel probably goes beyond the author's intentions to become a primer of masculine metaphysics.

14. Ursula K. Le Guin, *The Dispossessed* (New York: Avon, 1974), p. 197.

15. Two wonderful books for prospective parents on this are by Thomas Verny, *The Secret Life of the Unborn Child* (New York: Summit Books, 1981), and Ashley Montagu, *Touching* (New York: Harper and Row, 1978).

16. Timothy Beneke, "Male Rage: Four Men Talk about Rape," *Mother Jones* VII (July, 1982), p. 20.
17. Nicholas Groth, *Men Who Rape: The Psychology of the Offender* (New York: Plenum Press, 1979).
18. Walter N. Pahnke and William A. Richards, "Implications of LSD and Experimental Mysticism," *The Journal of Transpersonal Psychology* 2 (1969), p. 89.
19. Ibid., p. 89.
20. John B. Cobb, Jr., *Christ in a Pluralistic Age* (Philadelphia: Westminster, 1975), p. 264.
21. Ibid., p. 263.
22. Kenneth Burke, "Version, Con-, Per-, and In-: Thoughts on Djuna Barnes's Novel *Nightwood*," *Southern Review* 11 (1966-67), pp. 329-346.

CHAPTER 3: The Nursing Mother and Feminine Metaphysics

1. Dorothy Dinnerstein, *The Mermaid and the Minotaur: Sexual Arrangements and Human Malaise* (New York: Harper and Row, 1976), p. 79.
2. Judith Ellen Plaskow, "Sex, Sin, and Grace: Women's Experience and the Theologies of Reinhold Niebuhr and Paul Tillich." Doctoral dissertation, Yale University, December 1975, p. 33.
3. Ibid., p. 33.
4. Ibid., p. 19.
5. Anne Sexton, *The Death Notebooks* (Boston: Houghton Mifflin, 1974), p. 31.
6. Ibid., p. 92.
7. Ibid., p. 97.
8. James Hillman, *The Myth of Analysis* (New York: Harper and Row, 1972).
9. Cited by Marina Warner, *Alone of All Her Sex: The Myth and Cult of the Virgin Mary* (New York: Knopf, 1976), p. 196.
10. Ibid.
11. Ibid., p. 197.
12. Sylvia Plath, *Ariel* (New York: Harper and Row, 1961), p. 1.
13. Wet-nursing is far too complex a phenomenon to be boiled down to one cause; its history is one long atrocity against chil-

dren and mothers. See Richard C. Trexler, "Infanticide in Florence: New Sources and First Results," *History of Childhood Quarterly* I (Summer 1973), pp. 99-116, and "The Foundlings of Florence, 1395-1455," *History of Childhood Quarterly* I (Fall 1973), pp. 259-284; also William L. Langer, "Infanticide: A Historical Survey," *History of Childhood Quarterly* I (Winter 1974), pp. 353-367; Lloyd Demause, "The Evolution of Childhood," *History of Childhood Quarterly* I (Spring 1974), pp. 503-576. An article that shows how the founders of the United States colonies rejected wet-nursing and so established better mother-child bonding is R. V. Schnucker's "The English Puritans and Pregnancy, Delivery and Breast Feeding," *History of Childhood Quarterly* I (Spring 1974), pp. 637-659.

14. Warner, *Alone of All Her Sex*, p. 203.
15. Euripides, *The Bacchae and Other Plays*, trans. Philip Vellacott (New York: Penguin, 1954), p. 196.
16. Toni Morrison, *Song of Solomon* (New York: New American Library, 1977), p. 13.
17. Edmund Spenser, *Poetical Works* (London: Oxford University Press, 1965), p. 53.
18. Susan Husserl-Kapit, "An Interview with Marguerite Duras," *Signs: Journal of Women in Culture and Society* II (Winter 1975), p. 434.

CHAPTER 4: The Older Woman as Matriarch

1. Carol Gilligan, "Women's Place in Man's Life Cycle," *Harvard Educational Review* 49 (November 1979), p. 442.
2. James Hillman, *The Myth of Analysis* (New York: Harper and Row, 1972), p. 250.
3. David Gutmann, "The Cross-Cultural Perspective: Notes Toward a Comparative Psychology of Aging," in James E. Birren and K. Warner Schaie, eds., *The Psychology of Aging* (New York: Van Nostrand Reinhold, 1977) vol. II, p. 320.
4. As quoted by Carolee Uits, recorder for a session entitled "Self-Image and Roles," in *No Longer Young: Work Group Reports from the 26th Annual Conference on Aging* (Detroit:

Wayne State University, 1974), p. 44. He goes on to say that post menopausal women are aggressive, but that if women are not passive during their child-rearing years, they cannot take care of the emotional development of young children. His opponent on the panel, Joan Israel, characterized these views as "hogwash" and said that women of all ages need to start developing stronger self-concepts. Gutmann is very influential in his field, and such statements as this one about the "goodness" of passive younger women suggests the unconscious hidden agenda of his work. Thus the polarizing of older men (whom he characterizes sometimes as feeling "castrated" in the face of older women) and women in his work may be reflecting his personal fantasy as well as the facts of his empirical research. His use of language often emphasizes polarization. What he calls passivity I would call patience and a receptive attitude toward the young child's development and unfolding.

5. Bernice L. Neugarten, *Personality in Middle and Later Life: Empirical Studies* (New York: Atherton, 1946), p. 47.

6. Marcia Westcott, "Feminist Criticism of the Social Sciences," *Harvard Educational Review* 49 (November 1979), p. 426.

7. David Gutmann, "Developmental Issues in the Masculine Mid-Life Crisis," *Journal of Geriatric Psychology* IX, p. 44.

8. D. M. Murphy, "Factors Related to the Self-Concept in the Aged: Relationship to Interview Data and Test Measure," Doctoral Dissertation, Loyola University of Chicago, 1975, p. 11.

9. Eva Kahana, "The Older Woman: Implications of Research for Social Policy," (unpublished paper), p. 4.

10. Kakusho Tachibana, "A Study of Introversion-Extraversion in the Aged," in *Social and Psychological Aspects of Aging*, eds. Clark Tibbitts and Wilma Donahue (New York: Columbia University Press, 1962), vol. I, pp. 655-656.

11. Marcello Cesa-Bianchi and Giancario Trentini, "A Future Contribution to the Study of Adjustment in Old Age," in *Social and Psychological Aspects of Aging*, eds. Clark Tibbitts and Wilma Donahue (New York: Columbia University Press, 1962), vol. I, pp. 623-627.

12. Gutmann, "Developmental Issues in the Masculine Mid-Life Crisis," p. 45.

13. Dr. Thompson is a respondent to Gutmann's article in the *Journal of Geriatric Psychology*, cited above, pp. 68-69.

14. See Nancy Chodorow, "Family Structure and Feminine Personality," in *Woman, Culture, and Society*, eds., Michelle Zimbalist Rosaldo and Louise Lamphere (Stanford: Stanford University Press, 1974), pp. 43-63.

15. Georgia Sassen, "Success Anxiety in Women: A Constructivist Interpretation of its Source and Significance," *Harvard Educational Review* 50 (February 1980), pp. 13-25.

16. Helena Znaniecki Lopata, "The Meaning of Friendship in Widowhood," in *Looking Ahead: A Woman's Guide to the Problems and Joys of Growing Older*, eds. Lillian E. Troll, Joan Israel, and Kenneth Israel (Englewood Cliffs, N.J.: Prentice Hall, 1977), pp. 93-105.

17. Kahana, "The Older Woman," p. 8.

18. Sandra E. Gibbs Candy, "What Do Women Use Friends For?" in *Looking Ahead*, pp. 106-111.

19. Beth B. Hess, "Life Course, Sex Roles and Friendship" (unpublished paper), p. 6.

20. Deborah Coleman Wolf, "Close Friendship Patterns of Older Lesbians," Dept. of Medical Anthropology, Anthropology Dept., University of California, San Francisco, California (unpublished paper), p. 4.

21. Ibid., p. 6.

22. Ann Holder and Marvin Ernst, "Single Sex Interaction: An Essential Choice for the Aging Widow" (unpublished paper), p. 7.

23. Hillman, *The Myth of Analysis*, p. 292.

24. Arlie Russell Hochschild, *The Unexpected Community* (Berkeley: University of California, 1973), pp. 94-97.

25. See my "Metaphysics of Matrilinearity in Women's Autobiography: Studies of Mead's *Blackberry Winter*, Hellman's *Pentimento*, Angelou's *I Know Why the Caged Bird Sings*, and Kingston's *The Woman Warrior*," *An Anthology of Criticism on Women's Autobiographies*, ed. Estelle C. Jelinek (Bloomington: Indiana University Press, 1980), pp. 180-206.

26. Gilligan, "Woman's Place," pp. 442, 444.

27. Toni Morrison, " 'Intimate Things in Place': A Conversation

with Toni Morrison," *Massachusetts Review* 18 (Autumn 1977), p. 488.

28. The goddesses are complex, many-sided figures, and I here select certain positive elements of Artemis. Some classicists emphasize her role as killer of women in childbirth; a few ancient poets blamed her for neglecting these women because she was too busy hunting. This is not a major interpretation of this goddess, but I mention it because I want the reader to realize that I am deliberately selecting the aspects of the goddesses that seem germane to the archetype I herein trace.

29. Vira R. Kivett, "Rural Frail Older Women: Implications of Policy and Planning," (forthcoming in *The Journal of Minority Aging*), p. 9.

30. Helena Znaniecki Lopata, "Living Arrangement of American Urban Widows," *Sociological Focus on Aging* V (Autumn 1971), p. 41. She emphasizes how many widows live alone and like it again in *Women as Widows: Support Systems* (New York: Elsevier, 1979), p. 54.

31. Margaret Feldman, "Filial Crisis Resolution by Adult Daughters" (unpublished paper), pp. 3, 15.

32. Murphy, "Factors Related to the Self-Concept in the Aged," p. 12.

33. Florida Scott-Maxwell, *The Measure of My Days* (New York: Knopf, 1973), pp. 12-13. There is work going on among critics of the visual arts that is complementary to this literary work. Two fine essays are by Estella Lauter and Dominique Rozenberg, "The Transformation of the Mother in Work of Käthe Kollwitz," *Anima* V (Spring 1979) pp. 83-99; and by Elizabeth Curry, "Käthe Kollwitz as Role Model for the Older Woman," *Chrysalis* 7 (1979), pp. 55-70.

34. Jon Hendricks and C. Davis Hendricks, *Aging in Mass Society: Myths and Realities* (Cambridge: Winthrop, 1977), p. 150. This is a textbook and so will make this concept more like "general knowledge."

CHAPTER 5: Old Age and Death

1. See Raymond A. Moody, *Life After Life* (New York: Bantam, 1976) for a popularized account. Elisabeth Kübler-Ross

has recently attested in interviews to personal out-of-body experiences.

2. Karlis Osis and Erlendur Haraldsson, *At the Hour of Death* (New York: Avon, 1977).

3. Robert E. Neale, "Between the Nipple and the Everlasting Arms," in *Death and Society*, eds. James P. Carse and Arleen B. Dallery (New York: Harcourt Brace Jovanovich, 1977), p. 436.

4. Ibid.

5. Judith M. Bardwick, *In Transition* (New York: Holt, Rinehart and Winston, 1979), p. 178.

6. Estella Lauter and Dominique Rozenberg, "The Transformation of the Mother in Work of Käthe Kollwitz," *Anima* V (Spring 1979), p. 90.

7. Elizabeth Curry, "Käthe Kollwitz as Role Model for the Older Woman," *Chrysalis* VII (1979), p. 69.

8. Kurt W. Back, "Metaphors as Test of Personal Philosophy of Aging," *Sociological Focus* V (Autumn 1971), pp. 1-8. Back is James B. Duke Professor of Sociology at Duke University; his other work is wide-ranging and reflects his concern for the failure of social science to provide spiritual paths and resources. See *Beyond Words: The Story of Sensitivity Training and the Encounter Movement* (New York: Russell Sage Foundation, 1972), pp. 213-219.

9. Paul Ramsey, "The Indignity of 'Death with Dignity'," *Death and Society*, eds. James P. Carse and Arleen B. Dallery (New York: Harcourt Brace Jovanovich, 1977), p. 126.

10. James Hillman, *The Dream and the Underworld* (New York: Harper and Row, 1979), p. 202.

11. Arlie Russell Hochschild, *The Unexpected Community* (Berkeley: University of California, 1973), p. 144; see also Patricia L. Kasschau, *Aging and Social Policy* (New York: Praeger, 1978), p. 402.

12. Neale, "Between the Nipple and the Everlasting Arms," p. 436.

13. Erich Neumann, *The Great Mother*, trans. Ralph Mannheim (Princeton: Princeton University Press, 1963), pp. 149-152.

14. Ashley Montagu, *Touching: The Human Significance of the Skin* (New York: Harper and Row, 1978), p. 259.

15. Diane McGuinness, "How the Schools Discriminate Against Boys," *Human Nature* 2 (February 1979), pp. 82-90.
16. Dorothy Dinnerstein's *The Mermaid and the Minotaur: Sexual Arrangements and Human Malaise* is a brilliant, widely read, but at times depressed and depressing Freudian rendition of this theory.
17. Mary Daly, *Gyn/Ecology: The Metaethics of Radical Feminism* (Boston: Beacon Press, 1978), p. 427.
18. Margaret Mead, *Blackberry Winter* (New York: William Morrow, 1972), p. 328.
19. Tillie Olsen, *Tell Me a Riddle* (New York: Dell, 1960), pp. 115-116.
20. Theodora Kroeber, *The Inland Whale* (Berkeley: University of California Press, 1959), pp. 35-36.
21. Florida Scott-Maxwell, *The Measure of My Days* (New York: Knopf, 1973), p. 149.
22. Ursula K. Le Guin, "The Day Before the Revolution" in *More Women of Wonder*, ed. Pamela Sargent (New York: Vintage, 1976), p. 289.
23. Edith Wharton, *The House of Mirth* (Boston: Houghton Mifflin, 1905), p. 310.
24. Toni Morrison, *Sula* (New York: Bantam, 1975), p. 128.
25. Robert Grinnell, *Alchemy in a Modern Woman* (Zurich: Spring Publications, 1973), p. 25.
26. Ibid., p. 2.
27. Anne Sexton, *45 Mercy Street*, ed. Linda Gray Sexton (Boston: Houghton Mifflin, 1976), p. 113.
28. Sylvia Plath, *Ariel* (New York: Harper and Row, 1961), p. 85.
29. Grinnell, p. 29.

CHAPTER 6: Accepting Femininity

1. S. E. Read, "The Maze of Life: The Work of Margaret Laurence," *Canadian Literature* 27 (Winter 1966), p. 10.
2. Margaret Laurence, *The Stone Angel* (New York: Knopf, 1964), p. 17.
3. Ibid., p. 292.

4.   Ibid., pp. 98-99.
5.   Ibid., p. 212.
6.   Ibid., p. 279.
7.   Ibid., p. 120.
8.   Ibid., p. 4.
9.   Ibid., p. 307.
10. Northrup Frye, *Literary History of Canada: Canadian Literature in English*, ed. Carl F. Klinck (Toronto: University of Toronto Press, 1965), p. 826.
11. Mary Daly, *Gyn/Ecology* (Boston: Beacon Press, 1978), p. 16.

CHAPTER 7: Femininity as Entrapment

1.   Mel Watkins, "Talk with Toni Morrison," *New York Times Book Review*, September 6, 1977, p. 50.
2.   Toni Morrison, *Song of Solomon* (New York: New American Library, 1977), p. 248.
3.   Ibid., p. 249.
4.   Ibid., pp. 249-250.
5.   Linda Leonard has authored a series of articles on the "puella," or woman fixated into the daughter role—an immature woman; most relevant to Ruth is "Puella Patterns," *Psychological Perspectives* IX (Fall 1978), pp. 127-147.
6.   Morrison, *Song of Solomon*, p. 320.
7.   Ibid., p. 335.
8.   Ibid., p. 149.
9.   Ibid., p. 150.
10. Many writers see this as the highest form of spirituality; see the recent excellent book by Jean Shinoda Bolen, *The Tao of Psychology: Synchronicity and the Self* (New York: Harper and Row, 1979), especially Chapter 8.
11. Morrison, *Song of Solomon*, p. 323.
12. Ibid., p. 40.
13. Ibid., p. 338.
14. " 'Intimate Things in Place': A Conversation with Toni Morrison," *Massachusetts Review* 18 (Autumn 1977), p. 485.
15. Morrison, *Song of Solomon*, p. 340.

16. Ibid., p. 340.
17. Peter Demetz, "The Elm and the Vine: Notes Toward the History of a Marriage Topos," *PMLA* LXXIII (1958), pp. 521-532.
18. I develop this image of woman's identification of her matrilineal roots as a tree in my book, "An Archetypal Analysis of Anne Sexton's Poetry: Toward a Feminine Experience of Godhead" co-authored with Estella Lauter, yet unpublished. A clinical psychologist who has studied depth images of female patients also finds that women identify their deepest selves with trees, Katherine Bradway, "Hestia and Athena in the Analysis of Women," *Inward Light* XLI (Spring 1978), p. 36. Another woman psychiatrist who analyzes this image is Jean Bolen, p. 70; she has also found the image useful with certain male patients, p. 47.
19. Morrison, *Song of Solomon*, p. 38.
20. Ibid., p. 46.

CHAPTER 8: Matriarch as Tender Ferocity

1. Paul Reboux calls Colette a pagan sensualist whose low level of consciousness kept her from espousing any religious concepts whatsoever; he is quoted by Anne A. Ketchum, *Colette ou la naissance du jour: Étude d'un malentendu* (Paris: Lettres Moderne Minard, 1968), p. 42. Also Ketchum quotes Réné Lalou from his *Histoire de la litterature française contemporaine* as saying that "l'art de Colette n'est inspiré que par la sensation," ("the art of Colette is only inspired by the senses"), p. 44. Andrew Therive says Colette's metaphysics consist of "la religion du néant" ("the religion of nothingness"), p. 52.
2. Colette, *My Mother's House and Sido*, trans. Una Vicenzo Troubridge and Enid McLeod (New York: Farrar, Straus and Giroux, 1953), p. 36.
3. Ibid., p. 5.
4. Ibid., pp. 23-25.
5. Ibid., pp. 117, 158, 166.
6. Ibid., p. 19.

7. Ibid., p. 79.
8. Ibid., p. 125.
9. Ibid., p. 152.
10. Ibid., p. 165.
11. Ibid., p. 201.
12. Ibid., p. 156.
13. Ibid.
14. Ibid., p. 171.
15. Ibid., p. 173.
16. Ibid., p. 166.
17. Ibid.
18. Ibid., p. 171.
19. Colette, *Break of Day*, trans. Enid McLeod (New York: Farrar, Straus and Giroux, 1961), p. 6.
20. Ibid., p. 141.
21. Ibid., p. 142.
22. Ibid., p. 93.
23. Colette, *The Evening Star*, trans. David Le Vay (London: Peter Owen, 1973), p. 102.
24. Ibid., p. 141.
25. Ibid., pp. 69-70.
26. Ibid., p. 21.
27. Yvonne Mitchell, *Colette: A Taste for Life* (New York: Harcourt Brace Jovanovich, 1975), p. 205.
28. Colette, *The Evening Star*, p. 95.
29. Ibid., p. 56.
30. Ibid., p. 68.
31. Colette, *My Mother's House and Sido*, p. 163.
32. Colette, *The Evening Star*, p. 53.
33. Ibid., p. 136.
34. Ibid., p. 144.
35. Colette, *Break of Day*, pp. 142-143.
36. Ibid., p. 64.
37. Ibid., p. 59.
38. Colette, *The Blue Lantern*, trans. Roger Senhouse (New York: Farrar, Straus and Giroux, 1963), p. 24.
39. Ibid., p. 58.
40. Ibid., p. 6.
41. Ibid., pp. 158-159.

42. Ibid., p. 161.
43. Maurice Goudeket, *Close to Colette* (New York: Farrar, Straus and Giroux, 1957), p. 31.
44. Ibid., p. 244.

CHAPTER 9: Symbols of the Feminine

1. Robert Grinnell, *Alchemy in a Modern Woman* (Zurich: Spring Publications, 1973), p. 20.
2. Penelope Shuttle and Peter Redgrove, *The Wise Wound: Eve's Curse and Everywoman* (New York: Richard Marek, 1978), see Chapter I.
3. Sylvia Plath, *Ariel* (New York: Harper and Row, 1961), p. 34.
4. Ellen Bass, "Tampons," *Chrysalis* (Fall 1979), pp. 47-49.
5. Colette, *The Evening Star*, p. 124.
6. Marc Edmund Jones, *How to Learn Astrology* (Boulder, Colorado: Shambhala Publications, 1941), p. 39.
7. Marc Edmund Jones, *The Guide to Horoscope Interpretation* (Wheaton, Illinois: The Theosophical Publishing House, 1941), p. 152.
8. William McGuire and R. F. C. Hull, eds., *C. G. Jung Speaking* (Princeton, N.J.: Princeton University Press, 1977), pp. 13-14, 30, 47-48.
9. Stephen Arroyo, *Astrology, Karma and Transformation* (Vancouver, Wash.: CRCS Publications, 1978), p. 121.
10. Dane Rudhyar, *The Astrology of Personality* (Berkeley: Doubleday, 1970), p. 261.
11. Liz Greene, *Relating: An Astrological Guide to Living with Others on a Small Planet* (Bungay, Suffolk: Richard Clay, 1978), p. 38.
12. Ibid., p. 39.
13. Ann and Barry Ulanov, *Religion and the Unconscious* (Philadelphia: Westminster Press, 1975), p. 154.
14. Carol Gilligan, "Woman's Place in Man's Life Cycle," *Harvard Educational Review* 49 (November 1979), p. 442.
15. Alice Bailey, *Esoteric Astrology* (London: Lucis Press, 1951), p. 448.
16. Ibid., p. 394.

17. Gloria Orenstein, "Leonora Carrington: Another Reality," *Ms.* III (August 1974), p. 31.
18. Ibid., p. 30.
19. This and the following paintings by Varos are in *Remedios Varos*, eds. Octavio Paz and Roger Caillois (Mexico, D.F.: Ediciones ERA, 1972). I am indebted to Estella Lauter for a lecture full of insights that she gave on Varos whose work I had not known previously.
20. A reproduction of this work by Judy Chicago is in *Ms.* III (May 1975), p. 64.
21. Adrienne Rich, *The Dream of a Common Language* (New York: Norton, 1978), pp. 406.

CHAPTER 10: Women's Spirituality and the Occult Tradition

1. James Hillman, "The Great Mother, her Son, her Hero and the Puer," in *Fathers and Mothers*, ed. Patricia Berry (Zurich: Spring Publications, 1973), p. 84.
2. Arthur Koestler, *The Roots of Coincidence* (New York: Random House, 1972), p. 19.
3. Martin Celnick and Robert Hogan, Letters to the Editor, *Psychology Today* 15 (October 1981), p. 6.
4. Michel Gauquelin, *The Cosmic Clocks: From Astrology to a Modern Science* (Chicago: Henry Regnery, 1967), p. 59.
5. Ted George, *The Lives You Live as Revealed in the Heavens: A History of Karmic Astrology and Pertinent Delineations* (Jacksonville, Fla.: Arthur, 1976), pp. 136-137.
6. Ian Stevenson, *Twenty Cases Suggestive of Reincarnation* (New York: American Society for Psychical Research, 1966), p. 130.
7. Ibid., pp. 180-182.
8. Ibid., pp. 130-131.
9. Ian Stevenson, "Some New Cases Suggestive of Reincarnation," *Journal of the American Society for Psychical Research* 66 (October 1972), p. 375.
10. Ruth Montgomery, *The World Before* (New York: Fawcett Crest, 1976), pp. 23-25.

11. Benjamin Creme, *The Reappearance of the Christ and the Masters of Wisdom* (London: Tara Press, 1980), p. 182.

12. Ibid., pp. 183-184.

13. Gina Cerminara, *Many Mansions* (New York: New American Library, 1950), p. 124.

14. Creme, *The Reappearance of the Christ*, pp. 184-185.

15. Cerminara, *Many Mansions*, p. 162.

16. Ibid.

17. Stevenson, *Twenty Cases*, p. 190.

18. Joan Grant and Denys Kelsey, *Many Lifetimes* (New York: Arno Press, 1980), p. 61.

19. George, *The Lives you Live*, pp. 7-8.

20. *Cosmic Awareness Speaks* II (Olympia, Wash.: Cosmic Awareness Communications, n.d.), pp. 59-60.

21. Montgomery, *The World Before*, p. 25.

22. *Revelations Awareness* (Olympia, Wash.: Cosmic Awareness Communications, 81-20, May 1981), p. 10.

23. Nicholas Regush, *The Human Aura* (New York: Berkley, 1974), p. 64.

24. "Newsline," *Psychology Today* 16 (March 1982), p. 23.

25. Regush, *The Human Aura*, p. 64.

26. Robert Van de Castle, abstract of "An Investigation of Psi Abilities Among the Cuna Indians of Panama," *Journal of Parapsychology* 38 (June 1974), pp. 231-232.

27. Robert Morris, abstract of his mass tests on junior high girls and boys in *Journal of the American Society for Psychical Research* 66 (April 1972), p. 214.

28. J. B. Rhine, *Extra-Sensory Perception* (Boston: Brandon, 1973), p. 207.

29. J. B. Rhine, "Security Versus Deception in Parapsychology," *Journal of Parapsychology* 38 (March 1974), p. 115.

30. Rhine, *Extra-Sensory Perception*, p. 216.

31. Karlis Osis and Mary Lou Carlson, "The ESP Channel — Open or Closed?" *Journal of the American Society for Psychical Research* 66 (July 1972), p. 314.

32. Siegfried Preiser, abstract of "Emotion versus Information — a Methodological Critique," in *Zeitschrift Fur Parapsychologie und Grenzgebiete der Psychologie* 15 (1973), pp. 171-186; also in *Journal of Parapsychology* 38 (March 1974), p. 129.

33. Ibid.
34. Adrian Parker, "Some Success at Screening for High-Scoring ESP Subjects," *Journal of the Society for Psychical Research* 47 (1974), pp. 366-370.
35. Osis and Carlson, "The ESP Channel," p. 310.
36. Jan Ehrenwald, "The Telepathy Hypothesis and Schizophrenia," *Journal of the American Academy of Psychoanalysis* 2(2): pp. 159-169 as abstracted in *Journal of Parapsychology* 47 (1974), p. 436. See also Rex G. Stanford and Brantz Mayer, "Relaxation as a Psi-Conducing State: A Replication and Exploration of Parameters," *Journal of the Society for Psychical Research* 68 (April 1974), pp. 182-192.
37. Jule Eisenbud, "Some Notes on the Psychology of the Paranormal," *Journal of the American Society for Psychical Research* 66 (January 1972), p. 39.
38. Ibid., p. 40.
39. Enid Hoffman, *Huna: A Beginner's Guide* (Rockport, Mass.: Para Research, 1981).
40. Naomi Goldenberg, *Changing of the Gods: Feminism and the End of Traditional Religions* (Boston: Beacon Press, 1979).
41. Gustav Theodor Fechner, *The Little Book of Life After Death*, trans. Mary C. Wadsworth (Boston: Little, Brown, 1904), pp. 25-28.
42. Scott Rogo, "Reassessing the Poltergeist," *Journal of Parapsychology* 43 (December 1979), p. 331.
43. Harmon H. Bro, *Edgar Cayce on Dreams* (New York: Warner Paperback Library, 1974), pp. 73-74.
44. Ibid.
45. Allan Angoff, *Eileen Garrett and the World Beyond the Senses* (New York: Eilliam Morrow, 1974), p. 78.
46. Ibid., p. 102.
47. James Albert Pike, *The Other Side* (New York: Doubleday, 1968).
48. Ruth Plant, *Journey into Light: An Account of Forty Years' Communication with a Brother in the After Life* (London: Cassell and Company, 1972).
49. Michelle Harrison, "Pre-Birth Communication," *Mothering* 16 (Summer 1980), p. 65.

CHAPTER 11: Morality and Matriarchal Wisdom

1. Robin Morgan, "Monster," *Monster* (New York: Random House, 1972), p. 82.
2. Lawrence Kohlberg, *The Philosophy of Moral Development: Moral Stages and the Idea of Justice* (San Francisco: Harper and Row, 1981), p. 348.
3. Ibid., p. 349.
4. Ibid., p. 170.
5. Ibid., p. 363.
6. Ibid., p. 371.
7. Ibid., p. 139.
8. Judith M. Bardwick, *In Transition* (New York: Holt, Rinehart and Winston, 1979), p. 132.
9. Kohlberg, *The Philosophy of Moral Develoment*, p. 403.
10. C. G. Jung, *Portable Jung*, ed. Joseph Campbell, trans. R. F. C. Hull (New York: Penguin, 1976), p. 561.
11. Jean Shinoda Bolen, *The Tao of Psychology*; see especially Chapter 8, "The Tao as Path with Heart."

Index

Stephanie Demetrakopoulos speaks and writes widely about women's image in society. An award-winning scholar and associate professor of women's studies at Western Michigan University, she traces the images of self that women generate in various art forms. By identifying hitherto unarticulated life-stage patterns unique to women, Demetrakopoulos develops a new feminine consciousness. A mother, wife, and teacher, she lives with her husband and children in Kalamazoo, Michigan.